HENRY DAVID THOREAU

Crayon portrait of Henry Thoreau by Samuel Worcester Rowse made in the summer of 1854 at about the time Walden *was published.* (Concord Free Public Library)

MAKERS OF AMERICA

HENRY DAVID THOREAU
A MAN FOR ALL SEASONS

DOUGLAS T. MILLER

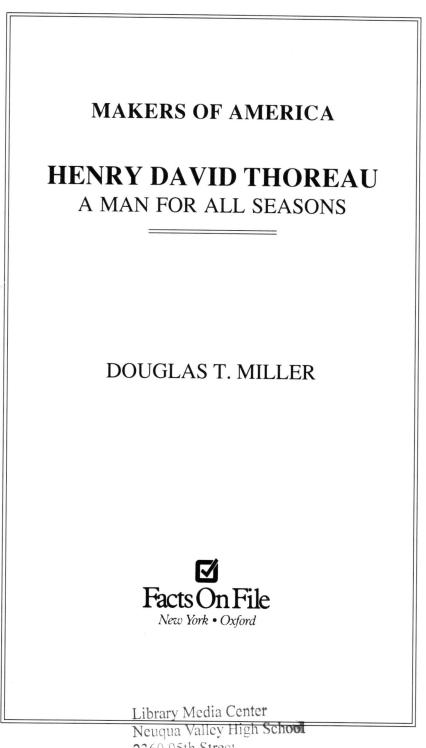

Facts On File
New York • Oxford

To my mother
and to my late father

Henry David Thoreau: A Man for All Seasons

Copyright © 1991 by Douglas T. Miller

All rights reserved. No part of this book may be reproduced or utilized in any form or by any means, electronic or mechanical, including photocopying, recording, or by any information storage or retrieval systems, without permission in writing from the publisher. For information contact:

Facts On File, Inc.
460 Park Avenue South
New York NY 10016
USA

Facts On File Limited
Collins Street
Oxford OX4 1XJ
United Kingdom

Library of Congress Cataloging-in-Publication Data

Miller, Douglas T.
    Henry David Thoreau / Douglas T. Miller.
        p.   cm. — (Makers of America)
    Includes bibliographical references and index.
    Summary: Presents the life and philosphies of this country's premier idealist.
    ISBN 0-8160-2478-2 (alk. paper)
    1. Thoreau, Henry David, 1817–1862—Biography. 2. Authors, American—19th century—Biography. [1. Thoreau, Henry David, 1817–1862. 2. Authors, American.] I. Title. II. Series: Makers of America (Facts on File, Inc.)
PS3053.M5   1991
818'.309—dc20
[B]   91–10787

British CIP data available on request from Facts On File.

Facts On File books are available at special discounts when purchased in bulk quantities for businesses, associations, institutions or sales promotions. Please contact the Special Sales Department of our New York office at 212/683-2244 (dial 800/322-8755 except in NY, AK, or HI).

Text design by Debbie Glasserman
Jacket design by Duane Stapp
Composition by Facts On File, Inc.
Manufactured by R. R. Donnelly & Sons
Printed in the United States of America

10 9 8 7 6 5 4 3 2 1

This book is printed on acid-free paper.

CONTENTS

PREFACE

Standing before a hushed audience crowded into the First Parish Church in Concord, Massachusetts on the afternoon of May 9, 1862, Ralph Waldo Emerson delivered a eulogy for his friend, Henry Thoreau, whose body lay in a coffin nearby: "The country knows not yet, or in the least part, how great a son it has lost." How true this would prove to be. Largely ignored in his lifetime, Henry Thoreau's fame and influence have grown to momentous proportions in the nearly century and a third since his death. His essay "Civil Disobedience" would inspire Mahatma Gandhi's Indian independence movement and Martin Luther King, Jr.'s nonviolent civil rights crusade. His classic work, *Walden*, would come to be recognized as the literary masterpiece of New England transcendentalism and one of America's great books.

Thoreau was a rebel who never accepted the world as presented to him. Writing to a friend just after Thoreau's death, David Shattuck, the president of Concord's bank, had this to say of him: "Mr. Thoreau was a man who never conformed his opinions after the model of others; they were his own; were also singular. Who will say they were not right? He had many admirers, and well he might for, whatever might be the truth of his opinions, his life was one of singular purity and kindness."

Thoreau was a sharp critic of America's acquisitive mainstream. He valued a simple life and lived close to nature. He hated slavery and fought against it throughout his life. But he was also appalled at how supposedly free people enslaved themselves in their pursuit of material possessions. He stood for freedom, privacy, and preservation of the environment, for work that had meaning and gave dignity, for spiritual communion with nature. One young admirer, Louisa May Alcott, predicted soon after his death that "though his life seemed too short, it would blossom and bear fruit for us long after he was gone." She prophesied correctly.

Indeed, it could be claimed that Thoreau speaks more for our age than for his own. The appeals of Thoreau for contemporary readers are many. To conservationists he is the pioneer ecologist living in harmony with the environment and fighting for the preservation of the wilderness. Friends of nature see him both as a kindred spirit and an inspiration. Lovers of literature celebrate his well crafted and often poetic prose; there is great beauty and even magic in *Walden*, and few who read it are unchanged by it. Critics of the contemporary scene of stock manipulations, junk bonds, and corporate takeovers identify with his scathing attacks on the burgeoning materialism of his own age. Reformers continue to utilize his tactics of nonviolent civil disobedience. Advocates of a simpler life see his philosophy as at least a partial panacea for today's ills. Some people, including this author, have quite literally followed his example and gone to the woods to build their own shelters.[1] Thoreau offers a valuable alternative vision of what life could be. He truly is a man for all seasons.

I first read *Walden* in the spring of my 13th year. My father, who greatly admired Thoreau and Whitman, had given me copies of *Walden* and *Leaves of Grass*. I devoured both that spring, often taking the two books with me as I canoed up the headwaters of the Passaic River in rural New Jersey. Where I lived, the Passaic was a white-water stream that had cut a deep gorge through the ancient Triassic lavas that form the Watchung Mountains. Working my way up the rapids was difficult, but a mile north the river became deep and slow moving. From that point I could easily paddle for several miles through pleasant countryside that was uninhabited except for a small riverside settlement known locally as Frog Hollow. Three miles beyond this I reached the river's main source—a wondrous wild area of oaks, dogwoods, high bush blueberries, and swampy lowlands. Often in the spring this region would flood, becoming a vast shallow lake dotted with tree- and bush-clad islands. Being on the Atlantic flyway, there were

---

[1]When Thoreau built his cabin in 1845, it cost him $28.12½. When I constructed a somewhat larger dwelling in 1974 it cost me $3,000.00.

usually thousands of ducks, geese, and other water birds. This was the Great Swamp and today, fortunately, it is a National Wildlife Refuge.

I vividly recall one warm day late that spring, when after having paddled into the center of the Great Swamp, I slapped the side of my green canvas canoe and then watched in awe as hundreds of startled ducks and geese burst aloft, nearly blackening the sky. Later that day, I let the canoe drift slowly down river as I read "Spring" and "Conclusion" from *Walden*. Although I have read these chapters many times since, and certainly with greater understanding, it is that first joyous encounter with the magic of Thoreau that I most remember.

A few years later I entered Colby College where I studied 19th-century American history, literature, and philosophy. I read Thoreau in a more scholarly manner, but with no less fascination. Living then in Maine also gave me an opportunity to climb Mount Katahdin and canoe the Penobscot and Allagash Rivers just as Thoreau had done many years before.

When I began work on my Ph.D. in the early sixties it was my intention to write a dissertation on Henry Thoreau. My mentor was not impressed and tried to persuade me that scholars had already exhausted this subject. Though not convinced, I did pick a different topic which led me away from the sage of Walden Pond.

Nevertheless, Thoreau continued to be a great influence in my life. Like many of my generation coming of age in the late 1950s and 1960s, I became active in the civil rights and peace movements. Thoreau's "Civil Disobedience" served as our bible, teaching us the powerful tactic of nonviolent resistance to the unjust and immoral policies of segregation and war.

Since becoming a professor in the mid-1960s, I have regularly assigned *Walden* and other writings of Thoreau. It has been thrilling over the years to see how deeply moved many students are on first experiencing Henry Thoreau.

In 1988, I published a biography of the 19th-century black leader Frederick Douglass in this *Makers of America* series. When asked by the General Editor, John Anthony Scott, if I would like to contribute another, I mentioned my long-standing interest in Thoreau. He was delighted. So, nearly three decades after being dissuaded from writing about this fascinating individual, my opportunity came. I've thoroughly enjoyed it.

Henry David Thoreau: A Man for All Seasons relies primarily on my reading and understanding of Thoreau's writings. My task has been made easier thanks to the numerous students of Thoreau who have preceded me. While the most influential scholars are discussed in the book's Epilogue and Selected Bibliography, special acknowledgment should be given here to the following Thoreauvians: Henry S. Canby, Wendell Glick, Walter Harding, William Howarth, Stanley Edgar Hyman, Joseph Wood Krutch, Richard Lebeaux, Melvin E. Lyon, James McIntosh, Michael Meyer, Sherman Paul, Joel Porte, Robert D. Richardson, Robert Sayre, Richard J. Schneider, J. Lyndon Shanley, Leo Stroller, and E. B. White.

Over the years many students, colleagues and friends have helped me clarify my ideas on Thoreau and New England transcendentalism. Earlier drafts of this book were read in whole or in part by David Bailey, Mary Bivens, David Guard, Joe Janeti, Nancy Miller, Billie Jean Moose, Frank Ochberg, and Harry Reed. Their suggestions were most helpful. My favorite cousin, Marcia Stern, who lives in Thoreau's Concord, was kind enough to take pictures of Walden Pond for me. I would also like to thank my editors, Tony Scott and James Warren, for encouraging me to write on Thoreau, making insightful editorial comments, and carefully copyediting the manuscript.

The research and writing of *Henry David Thoreau* has been assisted by two grants from Michigan State University which provided released time from teaching.

I wish to thank my mother, Nancy Taylor Miller, and to acknowledge my late father, Harold Elwell Miller. They helped instill in me a great love of nature and allowed me the freedom to explore the wilds in my very Thoreauvian childhood. To them this book is dedicated.

Finally, I am most indebted to my wife, Susanne Elin Nielsen Miller. We approach Thoreau from different perspectives; she is a literary critic, while I am a cultural historian. She read and reread every chapter and time and again asked the right questions and came forth with most valuable suggestions. In addition, she was a cheerful and loving companion throughout.

DOUGLAS T. MILLER
Mason, Michigan

HENRY DAVID THOREAU

1

BUILDING A HOME

The most interesting dwellings in this
country, as the painter knows, are the most
unpretending, humble log huts and cottages
of the poor commonly; it is the life of the
inhabitants whose shells they are and not
any peculiarity in their surfaces merely,
which make them *picturesque*; and equally
interesting will be the citizen's suburban
box, when his life shall be as simple and as
agreeable to the imagination, and there is as
little straining after effect in the style of his
dwelling.

—*Walden*

America in the 1840s was an aggressive, boisterous place.
"Life consists in motion," noted an astonished European
visitor. "The United States," this observer continued,
"presents certainly the most animated picture of universal
bustle and activity of any country in the world. Such a thing
as rest or quiescence does not even enter the mind of an
American."

The nation was in the throes of an incredible material and
physical expansion. Times were rapidly being altered by
steamboats, railroads, the telegraph, factories, and the growth
of cities. Many younger people, lured by the promise of pros-
perity, fled family farms and small towns for industrial or
commercial jobs in cities like Boston and New York. Others
sought a new life in the frontier West. In the South, an expand-
ing plantation economy based on slave labor held the key to
wealth. The times favored risk and gambling, and almost
everyone was out to get rich. As the noted Unitarian clergyman

William Ellery Channing observed: "How widely spread is the passion for acquisition, not for simple subsistence, but for wealth! What a rush into all departments of trade." "Go *ahead*," exclaimed another contemporary, "is the real motto of the country, and every man does push on, to gain in advance of his neighbour."

Indicative of the nation's expansive mode was the election of James K. Polk to the presidency in November of 1844. Polk championed America's "Manifest Destiny" to create an "empire of liberty" stretching from the Atlantic to the Pacific. On taking office in March of 1845, he initiated policies that in little more than a year would lead to the Mexican War and the seizing of millions of acres of Mexican land. That same month, a young man in Concord, Massachusetts, opted out of the rat race. His name was Henry David Thoreau, a 27-year-old Harvard graduate who had been variously employed as a teacher, a pencil maker, and a handyman. His ambition was to be a writer, and to further that career he sought to simplify his life and gain more solitude.

In late March he began construction of a cabin in the woods near the shore of Walden pond, a lovely glacial lake about two miles southeast of Concord village in Massachusetts. On land owned by his friend, philosopher Ralph Waldo Emerson, and with an ax borrowed from another philosophical friend, Bronson Alcott, Thoreau began cutting white pines to frame his new house.

> It was a pleasant hillside where I worked, covered with pine woods, through which I looked out on the pond, and a small open field in the woods where pines and hickories were springing up. The ice in the pond was not yet dissolved though there were some open spaces, and it was all dark colored and saturated with water. There were some slight flurries of snow during the days that I worked there; but for the most part when I came out on the railroad, on my way home, its yellow sand heap stretched away gleaming in the hazy atmosphere, and the rails shone in the spring sun, and I heard the lark and pewee and other birds already come to commence another year with us. They were pleasant spring days, in which the winter of man's discontent was thawing as well as the earth, and the life that had lain torpid began to stretch itself. . . . So I went

on for some days cutting and hewing timber, and also studs and rafters, all with my narrow ax.

More than a decade before Thoreau began construction of his cabin, American architects had invented an efficient technique for erecting houses—the balloon frame. Introduced in Chicago in 1833, this new system framed houses with precut, evenly spaced, light, two-by-four inch studs. Balloon framing soon revolutionized the housing industry and made possible mass produced and reasonably priced homes. Whether Thoreau was aware of this technique is not known. But had he been, it is doubtful he would have favored this method over the traditional timber-framing. Not only was he familiar with timber-framing but he liked its sturdiness and the simple honesty of its nailless, mortised and tenoned joints.[1]

By mid-April, Thoreau had cut and hewed the necessary posts, beams and lintels, and chiseled and assembled the mortised and tenoned joints. Early in May, after having dug a cellar six feet square by seven feet deep, which was later used to store potatoes, he adopted the age-old custom of inviting friends and neighbors to help raise the frame. Among those present on this auspicious occasion were Emerson, Alcott, Thoreau's close friend Ellery Channing, and his favorite Concord farmer, Edmund Hosmer, and his sons. "No man," claimed Thoreau, "was ever more honored in the character of his raisers than I."

With the frame in place, Thoreau returned to his solitary labors. For $4.25 he had purchased a shanty from an Irish worker, James Collins. He dismantled this shack and took the boards back to his pondside in small cartloads. There he spread each board on the grass to be bleached and warped back into square by the sun. With this symbolic act of purification complete, he used these boards to sheath and roof his hut. Sometime later he nailed shingles over the sheathing, thereby making his cabin impervious to rain. While working on his home he also cleared the adjacent briarfield and planted two and a half acres with beans, potatoes, corn, peas, and turnips.

---

[1] A tenon is a projection from a timber that fits precisely into a mortised hole in another timber. These are held together with a wooden peg. In Thoreau's case he used white pines for his framing members, but found the limbs of the honey locust tree made the best pegs.

By late June, except for a fireplace, chimney, lath and plaster, all of which were later added in the fall, Thoreau's handcrafted cabin was complete. It was, he claimed, "a tight shingled and plastered house, ten feet wide by fifteen long, and eight-feet posts, with a garret and a closet, a large window on each side, two trap doors, one door at the end, and a brick fireplace opposite." At the

Drawing of Thoreau's Walden cabin by his sister Sophia. (Author's collection)

back was a separate woodshed. Further removed was an outhouse. The pond served as his bathtub and supplied his drinking water, except during the summer months when he preferred the cooler water of a nearby spring.

Like the outside, the inside furnishings were simple, "consisting of a bed, a table, a desk, three chairs, a looking-glass three inches in diameter, a pair of tongs and andirons, a kettle, a skillet, and a frying-pan, a dipper, a wash-bowl, two knives and forks, three plates, one cup, one spoon, a jug for molasses, and a japanned lamp."

The completed cabin, according to Thoreau's precise calculations, cost him $28.12½, nearly $2.00 less for a permanent house than the $30.00 a year he had been obliged to pay for a small dormitory room at Harvard College a few years earlier. He was delighted, as was his friend Channing who described Thoreau's abode in glowing terms: "It was just large enough for one. . . . It was . . . a sentry-box on the shore, in the wood of Walden, ready to walk into in rain or snow or cold. . . . It was so superior to the common domestic contrivance that I do not associate it with them. By standing on a chair you could reach into the garret, and a corn broom fathomed the depth of the cellar. It had no lock to the door, no curtain to the window, and belonged to nature as much as to man."

American architecture at the time Thoreau built his house was becoming increasingly ostentatious. The simple colonial, Georgian, and Greek revival styles were giving way to Victorian Gothic. Everywhere successful Americans, eager to show off their newly acquired wealth, were erecting lavish houses designed to impress. Function was subordinated to visual effect. False fronts, nonfunctioning windows, pillars, turrets, and gingerbread trim proliferated as people sought to outdo one another.

To Thoreau all this was nonsense:

> Most men appear never to have considered what a house is, and are actually though needlessly poor all their lives because they think that they must have such a one as their neighbors have.

True beauty in architecture, he believed would be that which

> has gradually grown from within outward, out of the character and necessities of the indweller and builder without even a thought for mere ornament, but an unconscious nobleness and truthfulness of character and life; and whatever additional beauty of this kind is destined to be produced will be preceded and accompanied, aye, created, by a like unconscious beauty of life . . . A great proportion of architectural ornaments are literally hollow, and a September gale would strip them off, like borrowed plumes, without injury to the substantials.

Thoreau also believed a man would have a far better appreciation of architecture if he built his own shelter. "There is," he declared, "some of the same fitness in a man's building his own house that there is in a bird's building its own nest. Who knows but if men constructed their dwellings with their own hands, and provided food for themselves and families simply and honestly enough, the poetic faculty would be universally developed, as birds universally sing when they are so engaged?"

The houses Thoreau admired were those whose forms were determined by needs and not by prior assumptions about what was beautiful. He believed the ideal dwelling should relate the inhabitants and their environment in a simple, organic way. "I wonder that houses are not oftener located mainly that they may command particular rare prospects, every convenience yielding to this." He had seen examples he admired: "the old-fashioned and unpainted" saltbox houses of Cape Cod, a simple miller's home in the Catskill Mountains "fit to entertain a travelling God," a woodsman's log cabin in the forests of Maine with "lichens and mosses and fringes of bark" for ornamentation.

His own house at Walden was also a modest example of his ideal. Made of local materials, sitting on a hillside with the front facing the sunny South and the pond, Thoreau's cabin was simply furnished and open to nature. In his writings he once described a somewhat grander vision of his model dwelling:

> I sometimes dream of a larger and more populous house standing in a golden age, of enduring materials, and without gingerbread work, which shall consist of only one room, a vast, rude, substantial, primitive hall, without ceilings or plastering, with bare rafters and purlins supporting a sort of lower heaven over one's head . . . A house whose inside is as open and manifest as a bird's nest.

Thoreau's cabin itself, and more importantly his writings about architecture, though largely ignored in his lifetime, would come to have a major influence on the development of modern architecture with its stress on organic structures and the need for the form of a building to be directly related to its function. Both Louis Sullivan and Frank Lloyd Wright, two seminal figures in the development of modern American architecture, read, admired and were inspired by Thoreau.

But why had Thoreau chosen to dwell alone away from society? Two days after he moved in he supplied an answer in his Journal: "July 6, 1845. I wish to meet the facts of life—the vital facts, which are the phenomena or actuality the Gods meant to show us—face to face, And so I came down here. Life! who knows what it is, what it does? If I am not quite right here, I am less wrong than before—and now let us see what they will have . . . Even time has a depth, and below its surface the waves do not lapse and roar." He chose the Fourth of July to move in, symbolically asserting his own independence.

Thoreau's aim was not to escape civilization, but to simplify it. As he wrote in *Walden*, his classic account of his years at the pond: "I wished to live deliberately, to front only the essential facts of life, and see if I could not learn what it had to teach, and not, when I came to die, discover that I had not lived. I did not wish to live what was not life, living is so dear . . ." He reduced his dependence on the world to a minimum, building his own house, raising and foraging for much of his food, and doing enough additional work to earn money for his immediate needs.

Though he enjoyed solitude and reveled in his new-found freedom at Walden, he had no desire to be a hermit. His house, which lay in sight of the road, was in easy walking distance of the village, and seldom did a day pass without Thoreau either visiting his family and friends in Concord or entertaining visitors at his pondside hut. Each Saturday his mother and sisters made a special trip to the pond, invariably bringing with them a welcomed home-cooked meal and on occasion clean laundry. Emerson and his family were also frequent visitors, as were the Alcotts and Channings.

Though just a child when Thoreau resided at Walden, Louisa May Alcott, later famous as the author of *Little Women*, recalled her parents' friend with great affection. He "used to come smiling up to his neighbors, to announce that the bluebirds had arrived, with as much interest in the fact as other men take in messages by the Atlantic cable."

In addition to entertaining his many friends, Thoreau, a great lover of nature, successfully tamed some of the wild animals living in the vicinity of his hut. Frederick Willis, who as a 17-year-old had visited Walden with the Alcotts, later recalled how Thoreau had led his guests outside the cabin and then

> gave a low curious whistle; immediately a woodchuck came running towards him from a nearby burrow. With varying note, yet still low and strange, a pair of gray squirrels were summoned and approached him fearlessly. With still another note several birds, including two crows, flew towards him, one of the crows nestling upon his shoulder. I remember it was the crow resting close to his head that made the most vivid impression upon me, knowing how fearful of man this bird is. He fed them all from his hand, taking food from his pocket, and petted them gently before our delighted gaze; and then dismissed them by different whistling, always strange and low and short, each little wild thing departing instantly at hearing its special sound.

Thoreau was especially fond of a field mouse that nested under his house. When he dined the mouse would come out and nibble morsels of food that he held in his fingers. After a time Thoreau could even summon the mouse by playing his flute, much to his visitors' delight, or at least the delight of those not squeamish of mice.

In warm weather the cabin became a favorite spot for picnics with sometimes as many as 25 of the townsfolk present. On August 1, 1846, during his second year at the pond, he hosted a meeting of the Concord Women's Anti-Slavery Society. Called to commemorate the freeing of the West Indian slaves, those assembled heard several speeches, including one by Emerson. The meeting ended with a pondside picnic lunch.

Thoreau's own meals, when he was not entertaining or dining out with friends, tended to be simple. He was largely a vegetarian, though he did enjoy fresh fish that he occasionally caught from the pond and nearby rivers, and once, angered at a woodchuck that had been devouring his garden, he killed and ate the animal, finding the meat quite tasty. He regularly baked a plain unleavened bread and soon got into the habit of adding raisins to it. For this, Thoreau has been credited with being the inventor of raisin bread.

Despite his active social life, Thoreau enjoyed long periods of solitude. He spent most of this time reading, writing and tending his garden, but above all else he loved to commune with nature. He became, in his own words, the "self-appointed inspector of snow-storms and rain-storms . . . surveyor, if not of highways, then of forest paths and all across-lot routes." On sunny mornings he often sat in his doorway listening to the birds singing round him, gazing in fascination at the colors in the pond, green in the depths, blue in the shallows. "I sit here at my window like a priest of Isis[2], and observe the phenomena of three thousand years ago, yet unimpaired. The . . .wild pigeons, an ancient race of birds, give a voice to the air, flying by twos and threes athwart my view or perching restless on the white pine boughs occasionally; a fish hawk dimples the glassy surface of the pond and brings up a fish."

Sometimes on quiet evenings he would row the small boat he had made to the center of the pond and play his flute for the lake's loons. His fascination with the pond did not cease in cooler weather. During his first winter at Walden he made a careful survey of the pond's size and depth. Local legend had it that Walden was bottomless; Thoreau not only accurately charted its bottom, but found that its deepest spot coincided with the pond's exact center.

Thoreau's afternoons were regularly spent exploring the countryside. Though the land about Walden and Concord was dotted with long-settled farms, Thoreau was adept at finding hidden and unexplored routes. He knew the area's fields, woodlots, swamps, streams, ponds, valleys, and hills far better even than their owners. "For my afternoon walks," he bragged,

> I have a garden, larger than any artificial garden that I have read of and far more attractive to me—mile after mile of embowered walks, such as no nobleman's grounds can boast, with animals running free and wild therein as from the first—varied with land and water prospect, and, above all, so retired that it is extremely rare that I meet a single wanderer in its mazes. No gardener is seen therein. You may wander away to solitary bowers and brooks and hills.

Thoreau was willing to share his natural world with friends, but on his terms. As one young companion noted, "to take a walk with Thoreau, one must rigidly adhere to the manners of

---

[2]Isis was the nature goddess worshipped in ancient Egypt.

the woods. He could lead one to the ripest berries, the hidden nest, the rarest flowers, but no plant life could be carelessly destroyed, no mother bird lose her eggs." Thoreau was quite picky in choosing walking partners, and once confessed in his Journal to having "met with but one or two persons in the course of my life who understood the art of taking walks daily—not to exercise the legs or body merely, nor barely to recruit the spirits, but positively to exercise both body and spirit, and to succeed to the highest and worthiest ends by the abandonment of all specific ends—who had a genius, so to speak, for sauntering."

Every aspect of nature held a fascination for Thoreau. He could spend hours squatting in a swamp watching muskrats build a house or a snapping turtle catch a fish. He was a naturalist and as adept at close observation and description as any scientist of his time. While at Walden he collected live specimens of fish and turtles, as well as a black snake and a mouse. He sent these to Louis Agassiz, a Swiss immigrant who had recently been appointed to head a new scientific school at Harvard. Thoreau was pleased when informed that among the fish he sent to Agassiz, who at the time was the most famous scientist in America, were two new species.

But while gifted as a scientist, Thoreau's interest in nature transcended mere observation and classification. To him nature was restorative. It was a cure for the ills of civilization: "I have come to this hill," he wrote in his notebook on one of his hikes, "to see the sun go down, to recover sanity and put myself again in relation with Nature." Or as he noted on another occasion: "It is important, then, that we should air our lives from time to time by removals, and excursions into the fields and woods—starve our vices."

Though he was absorbed by the specific facts of nature, his ultimate aim was to find a spiritual meaning underlying observable detailed data. In a beautiful passage from *Walden* he wrote: "Time is but the stream I go a-fishing in. I drink at it; but while I drink I see the sandy bottom and detect how shallow it is. Its thin current slides away, but eternity remains. I would drink deeper; fish in the sky, whose bottom is pebbly with stars." His real profession, he asserted, was "to be always on the alert to find God in nature, to know his lurking places, to attend all the oratorios, the operas, in nature." Thus, what seemed to his townspeople to be wasted time spent walking in the woods, was for Thoreau an intense search for spiritual truths.

When Frank Sanborn moved to Concord in 1855, he was told there were three religious groups in town—the Unitarians, the Orthodox and the Walden Pond Society. The latter, he was informed, were those who spent their Sundays walking about Walden absorbed in the beauties of nature. For Thoreau there was much truth in this observation. He had no use for churches or any distinctly Christian doctrines. Yet, he was highly religious and once proclaimed that "what in other men is religion is in me love of nature."

While nature served as a source of spiritual renewal for Thoreau, it was also the inspiration for his writing. With the leisure that his simple life at Walden afforded him he was able to spend several hours daily at his handcrafted desk. Much of his writing was in the Journal he had begun keeping soon after graduating from Harvard College in 1837. In it he expanded on his thoughts and observations made in the field. He also reflected on his current reading, quoted long passages and wrote nature sketches, poetry and his thoughts on a variety of topics. Keeping a daily Journal helped Thoreau learn the art of writing well. The Journal, which became a major part of his life's work, would also serve as the raw material for his various lectures, essays and books.

The years at Walden were incredibly productive. In addition to his voluminous journal writing, Thoreau completed drafts of the only two books he would see published during his lifetime: *A Week on the Concord and Merrimack Rivers* and *Walden*. He also wrote an important essay on the English author Thomas Carlyle and an account of a trip he took to the Maine woods: "Ktaadn." This was a time of great personal growth for Thoreau as well. His life was rich and insightful, and he was able to provide a sustained record of that life in a most beautiful literary style.

On September 6, 1847, exactly two years, two months and two days after he had moved in, Thoreau left Walden. As he explained:

> I left the woods for as good a reason as I went there. Perhaps it seemed to me that I had several more lives to

live, and could not spare any more time for that one. It is remarkable how easily and insensibly we fall into a particular route, and make a beaten track for ourselves. I had not lived there a week before my feet wore a path from my door to the pondside; and though it is five or six years since I trod it, it is still quite distinct.

At Walden Pond, Thoreau learned a wise approach to life, one which would remain with him the rest of his days. As he proclaimed in *Walden*:

I learned this, at least, by my experiment: that if one advances confidently in the direction of his dreams, and endeavors to live the life which he has imagined, he will meet with a success unexpected in common hours. He will put some things behind, will pass an invisible boundary; new, universal, and more liberal laws will begin to establish themselves around and within him; or the old laws be expanded, and interpreted in a more liberal sense, and he will live with the license of a higher order of beings. In proportion as he simplifies his life, solitude will not be solitude, nor poverty poverty, nor weakness weakness.

Thoreau's success at Walden was personal and would have been judged a failure by most of his money-mad contemporaries. He was indifferent to their judgment. "If the day and the night," he wrote, "are such that you greet them with joy, and life emits a fragrance like flowers and sweet-scented herbs, is more elastic, more starry, more immortal,—that is your success."

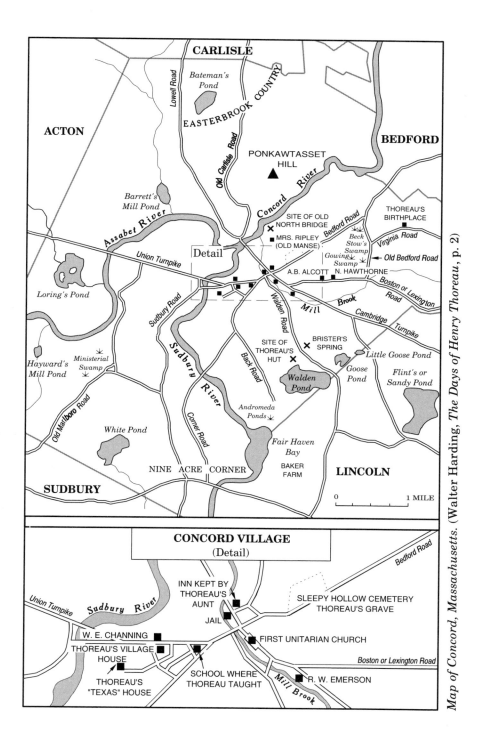

CARLISLE

Bateman's Pond

Lowell Road

EASTERBROOK COUNTRY

Old Carlisle Road

ACTON

BEDFORD

PONKAWTASSET HILL ▲

Concord River

Barrett's Mill Pond

Assabet River

SITE OF OLD NORTH BRIDGE ✕

MRS. RIPLEY (OLD MANSE) ■

Bedford Road

THOREAU'S BIRTHPLACE

Beck Stow's Swamp

Virginia Road

Union Turnpike

Detail

A.B. ALCOTT ■ N. HAWTHORNE

Gowing Swamp ← Old Bedford Road

Loring's Pond

Walden Road

Mill Brook

Boston or Lexington Road

Cambridge Turnpike

Sudbury Road

Sudbury River

SITE OF THOREAU'S HUT ✕

BRISTER'S SPRING ✕

Little Goose Pond

Hayward's Mill Pond

Ministerial Swamp ↓

Back Road

Walden Pond

Goose Pond

Flint's or Sandy Pond

Old Marlboro Road

Corner Road

White Pond

Andromeda Ponds ↓

Fair Haven Bay

NINE ACRE CORNER

BAKER FARM

LINCOLN

SUDBURY

0 ⸺⸺⸺⸺⸺ 1 MILE

CONCORD VILLAGE
(Detail)

Bedford Road

Union Turnpike

Sudbury River

INN KEPT BY THOREAU'S AUNT ■

JAIL

SLEEPY HOLLOW CEMETERY THOREAU'S GRAVE

W. E. CHANNING ■

FIRST UNITARIAN CHURCH ■

THOREAU'S VILLAGE HOUSE ■

Boston or Lexington Road

SCHOOL WHERE THOREAU TAUGHT ■

Mill Brook

R. W. EMERSON ■

THOREAU'S "TEXAS" HOUSE ■

Map of Concord, Massachusetts. (Walter Harding, The Days of Henry Thoreau, p. 2)

2
THE EARLY YEARS

> I came into this world, not chiefly to make
> this a good place to live in, but to live in it,
> be it good or bad.
>
> —*Walden*

Thoreau was born on July 17, 1817, in his grandmother's farmhouse on Virginia Road just at the outskirts of Concord village. His ancestry was French on his father's side, Scottish and English on his mother's. Three months after his birth, Dr. Ezra Ripley, Concord's best known minister, christened the young child David Henry Thoreau. His parents and friends always called him Henry and soon after his 20th birthday he chose to reverse his given names.

John Thoreau, Henry's father, was born in Boston in 1787 and moved to Concord in 1812, the same year that he married Cynthia Dunbar. He was a short, prematurely balding man with a large nose characteristic of the Thoreau family. He had kind eyes, spoke in a gentle voice, and was well liked by his neighbors. He was also well-read and enjoyed playing the flute. But having little ambition and no head for business, he failed in various enterprises, including several storekeeping ventures. At the time of Henry's birth the family was poor even by the modest standards of the time.

Henry's mother, Cynthia, was the more vivacious and dynamic of his parents. A large, attractive woman with high social aspirations, she dominated the household. In Concord she was well known as a great talker and holder of strong opinions. Active in civic affairs, she was a member of the Concord Female Charitable Society and the Bible Society, and in the 1830s would become one of the founders of the Concord

Women's Anti-Slavery Society. Henry's parents appear to have had a close relationship and shared a concern for the family and a love of nature. Besides Henry, the family consisted of a sister, Helen, and a brother, John, who were five and two years older, respectively. A second sister, Sophia, was born in 1819.

The Thoreaus were a tight-knit family. Poverty did not prevent the parents from creating a comfortable and support- ive homelife for their children. Soon after Henry's birth, they moved to nearby Chelmsford, and then to Boston. Economic misfortunes continued to plague the Thoreaus until the family moved back to Concord in 1823. There Henry's father began a modestly successful pencil-making business. To supplement their income the Thoreaus took in boarders; through most of Henry's childhood, besides his immediate family, the house- hold consisted of a number of maiden aunts, spinsters and widows, as well as a lovable eccentric uncle. It was a crowded, noisy home ruled by women. Henry often sought the solitude of his garret room or of nature.

Concord had been settled by the Puritans in the 1630s. During Thoreau's boyhood it was a pleasant New England village with tree lined streets, white clapboard houses, and some 2,000 inhabitants. It was a proud community which could boast of having launched the American Revolution when on April 19, 1775, the brave Minutemen, a collection of ill-trained farmers, boys as well as old men, attacked a regiment of British regulars on the town's North Bridge. After the Revolution the battle at the bridge assumed mythic dimensions. Americans celebrated the patriots who dared death at "the rude bridge that arched the flood" and "fired the shot heard 'round the world."

Twenty miles northwest of Boston, the town was located on the plains surrounding the juncture of the Assabet and Sud- bury Rivers which form the Concord River. Beyond the rivers were low glaciated hills, among which nestled a number of ponds and swamps. Situated on the main roads connecting Boston to western Massachusetts and southern New Hamp- shire, Concord's hotels and stores served the needs of travelers. There were a few small industries in town, but mainly it was a quiet, rural community with forests and fields never far away.

As many other small town boys, Henry was fascinated by the nearby countryside. He and his older brother, John, spent much of their youth exploring Concord's woods and meadows. They enjoyed fishing and hunting, though the younger brother soon gave up the gun and came to hate killing. In 1833, Henry, who was already a good craftsman, built a rowboat that he named *The Rover*. In this he spent endless hours paddling and drifting on Concord's meandering streams and clear glacial ponds. In winter these same streams and ponds provided mile after mile of pleasurable skating. Henry would later describe his childhood as an "ecstasy" and Concord "the most estimable place in all the world."

School came as a rude interruption to life's real pleasures. Henry was first sent to Phoebe Wheeler's private "infant" school which was held in an old Concord house on Walden Street. Soon after, he was enrolled in the public grammar school, a fairly typical one-room schoolhouse, where children of varying ages, grades and abilities were thrown together. Henry Thoreau was a good student; somewhat shy and solemn with his classmates, he seldom participated in their organized games, parties and pranks. This behavior earned him the nickname "Judge."

In the fall of 1828, the year Andrew Jackson was first elected to the presidency, the 11-year-old Henry and his brother, John, were enrolled in Concord Academy. Founded in 1822 as a private school for boys, the aim of the Academy was to prepare young men to enter Harvard College. Here under the tutelage of Phineas Allen boys were drilled in Greek, Latin, French, mathematics, history, geology, and natural history. Henry also learned to play the flute at this time, an instrument he would enjoy the rest of his life.

The Thoreau brothers graduated from the Academy in 1833. Many considered the outgoing John the more promising of the two. But clearly Henry was the better scholar, and it was he whom the family decided to enroll in Harvard since their finances would not allow them to send both. As it was, all the family members had to sacrifice to raise the nearly $180 it took at that time to pay for a year at Harvard. Henry did well enough to be awarded a much needed $25 scholarship at the end of his first year, and fortunately continued to win such support throughout his college years.

Harvard, though America's oldest and best known college, was not particularly distinguished during the years that Thoreau was in attendance, 1833–1837. Its liberal arts curriculum had been changed very little since colonial times. The emphasis was on the classics, mathematics, English, history, and modern languages. Although the college had introduced a few elective courses beginning in 1825, the faculty discouraged students from taking these by allowing them only half the usual credit. Teaching methods of the day stressed rote memorization and discouraged original thinking. The college also had dress codes, strict hours, and required attendance at chapel. It is no wonder then, that most students despised the system. The most violent rebellion in Harvard's history occurred during Thoreau's freshman year. Several days of student rioting led to the expulsion of the entire sophomore class.

Although Thoreau did not participate in the Great Rebellion, he shared many of his classmates' criticisms of the system. When later in his life he overheard Emerson remarking to a young admirer that Harvard taught all branches of learning, Thoreau quipped: "Yes, indeed, all the branches and none of the roots."

Yet Harvard had a major influence on Thoreau's intellectual growth. For one thing, he mastered a number of foreign languages. Always adept at language study, Thoreau emerged from Harvard with the ability to read Greek, Latin, Italian, French, German, and Spanish. This gave him both access to the major classics of Western civilization and familiarity with a variety of different cultures.

Nor did he neglect his study of nature while at Harvard. Though Cambridge, the town in which the college is located, stood just across the Charles River from the bustling metropolis of Boston, it was still largely a rural community. When not reading or in class, Henry often wandered along the banks of the Charles and observed the wildlife. One winter he was fortunate to find the home of an ermine in the hollow of an apple tree. He visited this site almost daily.

Harvard also helped turn Thoreau into a scholar. He became accustomed to systematic study and above all to using the library. Though small by modern standards, Harvard's collection of over 50,000 books was one of the great repositories of learning at the time. Thoreau took advantage of it and continued to borrow books from the college throughout his life. Not long before his death, he told Emerson's son, Edward, then about to begin at Harvard, that the library was the finest resource the college had to offer. However, Harvard was not the only great influence on Henry Thoreau during these years. Orestes A. Brownson and Ralph Waldo Emerson became two seminal figures in terms of his intellectual development.

In November of 1835, the Harvard faculty adopted a plan to assist poorer students. The program allowed these scholars to earn extra money by teaching outside the college for a term. Almost immediately the impoverished Thoreau took advantage of this. When the new term began that December he was off to teach in Canton, Massachusetts, having been hired by the Rev. Brownson, the Unitarian minister there. When Thoreau arrived Brownson agreed to put him up. That first night Brownson and Thoreau talked until midnight. They quickly became friends and soon commenced studying German together.

Orestes Brownson was no ordinary country clergyman. About 33 years old at the time Thoreau met him, he was a brilliant intellectual and a radical reformer who believed that organized religion should be a force for social change. He was also one of the sharpest critics of the emerging factory system and the growing inequalities between capitalists and workers. Like his European contemporary, Karl Marx, Brownson realized that a person operating a machine owned by another was in an inherently unequal position. Like Brownson, Thoreau would come to be a sharp critic of the new factory system which he believed ruthlessly exploited the worker.

Though Thoreau's stay with Brownson lasted only a month and a half, it was an intense period of intellectual growth for the impressionable young Harvard student. Night after night the two stayed up discussing philosophy, literature, religion, and reform. Two years later, Thoreau confided in a letter to Brownson that the "six weeks which I passed with you ... were an era in my life—the morning of a new *Lebenstag* [life]. They are to me as a dream that is dreamt, but which returns from time to time in all its original freshness. Such a one as I would dream a second and third time, and then tell before breakfast."

Back at Harvard after his brief teaching stint, Thoreau returned to his studies. But in the spring of 1837, while browsing through the college library he chanced upon a slim volume entitled *Nature* by Ralph Waldo Emerson. Henry Thoreau was fascinated. He read the book, then reread it, then went out and bought his own copy and another for one of his classmates. *Nature* had a profound impact on the young man about to graduate and go out in the world.

Generally speaking people are most moved by those books that express ideas for which they already have an affinity. Certainly this was the case with Thoreau. One can imagine his thrill on reading the opening lines of *Nature*:

> To go into solitude, a man needs to retire as much from his chamber as from society. I am not solitary whilst I read and write, though nobody is with me. But if a man would be alone, let him look at the stars.

Ralph Waldo Emerson in 1838. (Author's collection)

Or further on where he read:

> The lover of nature is he whose inward and outward senses
> are still truly adjusted to each other; who has retained the
> spirit of infancy even into the era of manhood. His inter-
> course with heaven and earth becomes part of his daily
> food.

At the time he read *Nature*, Thoreau had a nodding acquaint-
ance with the author. In 1834, Emerson, then 31 and a graduate
of both Harvard College and Harvard Divinity School, had moved
to Concord. The following year Thoreau was among a group of
Harvard students whom Emerson examined on rhetoric. There
is no record of this meeting, but perhaps Thoreau made a favorable impression, as Emerson, just before Henry's graduation,
wrote to Harvard's president on his behalf recommending that
the college extend further financial aid. But while in later years
these two would become close friends, in 1837 it was the book
Nature and not the man Emerson that captivated Thoreau.

Nature was much more than a celebration of the wild. It was
the radical manifesto of a new philosophical movement known as
transcendentalism. During the 1830s a small group of younger
intellectuals came to challenge the various orthodoxies of the day.
Drawing from German philosophical idealism and the English
authors Thomas Carlyle and Samuel Taylor Coleridge,[1] the
American transcendentalists came to believe that every individual had the intuitive power to grasp divine and universal truths.
The physical universe that one experienced through the senses
was, for the transcendentalists, mere appearance. Underlying
the material world was a deeper spiritual reality that could only
be comprehended through intuition.

In addition to Emerson, early exponents of transcendentalism included Orestes Brownson, Emerson's cousin George Rip-

---

[1]Emerson had recently met these English romantic writers who had been
particularly influenced by the German philosopher Immanuel Kant. From
Kant they learned the shortcomings of the scientific method of relying only
on sense experience and reason. Science, Kant believed, could never be more
than probable since it could only understand the material world. Higher
religious and moral concepts such as goodness, justice, beauty and God were
not material and consequently could not be understood by the methods of
science. Only through intuitive means, Kant argued, could one comprehend
these higher transcendent truths.

ley, Theodore Parker, Margaret Fuller, and Elizabeth and Sophia Peabody. These people had been raised in the liberal Unitarian church and many of them, like Emerson, were or had been Unitarian ministers.[2] But they came to find Unitarianism to be too rational and too institutionalized. True religion, they believed, needed neither church nor clergy. It could be experienced in nature by anyone willing to open themselves up and perceive the divinity of all. As Emerson wrote in a famous passage in *Nature*: "Standing on the bare ground,—my head bathed by the blithe air, and uplifted into infinite space,—all mean egotism vanishes. I become a transparent eyeball; I am nothing; I see all; the currents of the Universal Being circulate through me; I am part or parcel of God."

For Thoreau, who had always found more solace and spirituality in nature than in society and its institutions, transcendentalism rang true. Here was a liberating creed with which one could challenge existing institutions, traditions and values. It was a radical doctrine that held each individual responsible for perceiving moral truths. At its core, transcendentalism stood for complete personal freedom. People should not live by creeds, forms or precedents, but freely and spontaneously in accordance with their own inner promptings.

By the time of his graduation in August, 1837, Thoreau had thoroughly digested the works of the transcendentalists. Soon he would become a welcomed member of the transcendental circle that centered about Emerson's house in Concord. But having a philosophy is one thing, choosing a career quite another.

Because of his high academic standing, Thoreau was asked to deliver a speech at his commencement exercises. He picked as his topic "The Commercial Spirit of Modern Times" and lashed out at those Americans who were slaves of avarice:

> Let men, true to their natures, cultivate the moral affections, lead manly and independent lives; let them make riches the means and not the end of existence, and we shall

---

[2]Unitarians rejected the doctrine of the Trinity and maintained that God was one being. They emphasized freedom in religious belief, tolerance of difference in religious opinion and reason as the best guide to moral conduct. This liberal theology was strongly influenced by the Enlightenment and had become the most important religious movement in the Boston-Cambridge-Concord region during the early 19th century.

hear no more of the commercial spirit . . . This curious world which we inhabit is more wonderful than it is convenient, more beautiful than it is useful—it is more to be admired and enjoyed then, than used. The order of things should be somewhat reversed,—the seventh should be man's day of toil, wherein to earn his living by the sweat of his brow, and the other six his sabbath of the affections and the soul, in which to range this wide-spread garden, and drink in the soft influences and sublime revelations of Nature.

Though influenced by Emerson and Brownson, in this speech Thoreau was finding his own voice. The convictions he expressed that graduation day remained with him throughout his life and would be one of the central themes of his masterpiece, *Walden*.

Interestingly, Emerson, too, spoke at Thoreau's graduation. He delivered his "American Scholar" address, calling for a truly American literature freed from the cultural ties of Europe. But while Thoreau would go on to help create such a literature, there is no evidence that he stayed to hear Emerson's famed literary Declaration of Independence. In all likelihood he was already headed back to Concord and pondering his future.

3

THE ROAD TO WALDEN

I only ask a clean seat. I will build my lodge
on the southern slope of some hill, and
take there the life the gods send me. Will
it not be employment enough to accept
gratefully all that is yielded me between
sun and sun?

— *Journal*, April 5, 1841

Henry Thoreau could not have picked a more difficult
time to launch a career. The American economy, which
had been booming for more than a decade, suddenly
went into a tailspin during the winter of 1837, Thoreau's senior
year at Harvard. In the industrializing North unemployment
became widespread. Financial panics resulted in bank closings
and the suspension of specie payments (gold and silver).
Worker protests were widespread. In New York City there was
a major food riot. In the South cotton prices plummeted, while
in the West the bottom dropped out of the once booming land
market. By the time Thoreau graduated in August, 1837, the
United States was in the midst of the worst depression in its
short history. Its effects would persist until about 1843. Meanwhile, jobs, even for college graduates, were scarce.

But Thoreau was lucky. On returning home to Concord he
was informed of an opening in the local school. Though his real
aim was to be a poet of nature, immediate necessity came first.
He applied for the position and was offered the job. He began
to teach that September. In the typical one-room schoolhouse
of the time discipline was a major problem. Most teachers relied
on the rod. Thoreau would have none of this and so informed
the school committee. At the end of his second week on the job

a member of that committee visited his classroom. Finding the class too unruly, he took Thoreau aside and insisted that the new teacher flog disruptive pupils "or the school would spoil." Thoreau returned to the classroom, randomly called forth six students and rapped their knuckles with a ruler. That evening he resigned.

Thoreau then began looking for a new teaching position. But though he inquired as far south as Virginia and even took a trip to Maine in search of employment, he found no openings. Finally, in June, 1838, he started his own private school in his parents' home. Within a few months the school was prospering sufficiently for Thoreau to invite his brother to join him. That September they moved into the Concord Academy building which had been vacant since the depression began. The school flourished and soon had a waiting list. Pupils came not only from Concord but from neighboring communities as well.

Several months before opening the school Henry had written to Brownson concerning his teaching philosophy: "I could make education a pleasant thing both to the teacher and the scholar. This discipline which we allow to be the end of life, should not be one thing in the schoolroom, and another in the street. We should seek to be fellow-students with the pupil, and we should learn of, as well as with him, if we would be most helpful to him. . . . I have ever been disposed to regard the cowhide as a nonconductor. Methinks that, unlike the electric wire, not a single spark of truth is ever transmitted through its agency to the slumbering intellect it would address."

Now with their own school the Thoreaus had the opportunity to put this progressive philosophy into practice. The result was one of America's happiest and most successful educational experiments. Students were offered the standard curriculum of the day. Henry taught Latin, Greek, French, physics, natural philosophy, and natural history; John handled the "English branches" and mathematics. The brothers also took students on hikes through the countryside and boat trips on the rivers. They searched for arrowheads, birds, and flowers. The teachers imparted their knowledge and love of nature; they told students about the Indians who once inhabited the area; the young scholars learned to respect the environment and were even taught to survey land, to repair boats, and to forage for food in the wild. There was much sharing and no beatings. Discipline was never a problem. As one of the students later recalled: "It was a peculiar school, there was never a boy flogged or threatened, yet I never saw so absolutely military discipline. How it was done I scarcely know. Even the incorrigible were brought into line." Boys and girls whose parents were too poor to pay tuition during these hard times were taught for free. Students thrived under this system and all those interviewed about the school in later years remembered it with great fondness.

During this period of the school Henry's one romance occurred. In July, 1839, shortly after Thoreau's 22nd birthday, Ellen Sewall, an attractive and vivacious girl of 17, came to Concord for a visit. Ellen's home was in Scituate, on the coast south of Boston, but her aunt, Prudence Ward, boarded with the Thoreaus as did her younger brother, Edmund, who was a student in the brothers' school. Almost immediately Henry fell in love, and five days after meeting Ellen wrote in his Journal: "There is no remedy for love but to love more."

In the several weeks of Ellen's visit both Henry and John escorted her about the countryside. They took her on walks to some of the brothers' favorite spots: Emerson Cliffs, Fairhaven and Walden Ponds. They rowed up the Assabet River and even marveled at a giraffe that a traveling troupe brought to Concord. "I can not tell you half I have enjoyed here," the young lady wrote to her parents. By the time she left both brothers were in love with her.

Soon after her departure the young men took a memorable two week boat trip on the Concord and Merrimack Rivers, an excursion that would become the framework for Thoreau's first book. But, clearly Ellen was on both of their minds, and almost as soon as they returned John hurried off to Scituate for a brief visit. The following June, Ellen returned to Concord and again the brothers vied for her affection. Henry took her rowing and later wrote in his Journal: "The other day I rowed in my boat a free—even lovely young lady—and as I plied the oars, she sat in the stern—and there was nothing but she between me and the sky."

John was the bolder of the brothers, and in July, 1840, he again journeyed to Scituate, this time to propose. At first Ellen accepted him, but then realizing that it was Henry whom she really loved, she changed her mind. With John no longer a rival, Henry himself proposed in a letter to Ellen that November.

This time her father forbade the marriage, believing Thoreau to be too radical. She wrote Henry a short letter of refusal. To her Aunt Prudence she confessed, "I never felt so badly at sending a letter in my life." Four years later she married a minister named Joseph Osgood.

Ellen Sewall about 1840. (Author's collection)

As for Henry, although he would have many affectionate relationships with both men and women, he would never marry. Some scholars have suggested that nature became for Thoreau a refuge from romantic rejection. Though there may be some truth in this, he frequently thought of Ellen in later life, and on his deathbed confessed to his sister, "I have always loved her."

While Thoreau failed at love, he did make a number of significant friends during these years. The most important was Emerson, who first befriended Thoreau in the fall of 1837 soon after Henry's graduation from college. Emerson, then 34, was 14 years Thoreau's senior and came to serve the younger man as a mentor and older brother. For his part Emerson was quite captivated by Henry. In his journal early in their relationship he confided: "I delight much in my young friend, who seems to have as free and erect a mind as any I have ever met." A week later he wrote, "My good Henry Thoreau made this else solitary afternoon sunny with his simplicity and clear perception . . . Everything that boy says makes merry with society, though nothing can be graver than his meaning."

The importance of this friendship for Thoreau was immense. Emerson at that time was at the height of his intellectual powers. He had published *Nature* and "The American Scholar" and was working on various essays, lectures and poems. A magnanimous man, Emerson was one of those rare individuals who seem to have a certain aura about them. For instance, when Thomas Carlyle first met him he described him as "a beautiful transparent soul." He attracted and encouraged younger intellectuals and helped make Concord the center of what would come to be known as the "American Renaissance."

He and Thoreau began taking walks and having long talks together. Emerson encouraged Henry to keep a journal and to write poetry, both of which Thoreau took up with enthusiasm. Emerson also made available to Thoreau his extensive private library and recommended particular books to him. But above all, it was Emerson who opened up to Thoreau the larger intellectual world of transcendentalism.

Since 1836, American transcendentalists had been meeting informally on a somewhat regular basis. With the publication of *Nature*, Emerson came to be recognized as the unofficial leader of the movement and the so-called "Transcendental Club" most frequently met in his house. In the fall of 1837, Thoreau began attending these gatherings. He found himself not only in agreement with the basic ideas of transcendentalism, but he also met a number of fascinating intellectuals. He came to know Margaret Fuller, a writer and pioneer feminist; Elizabeth Peabody, an innovative educator and proprietor of a Boston bookstore where various free thinkers congregated; Theodore Parker, a Unitarian clergyman and outspoken abolitionist; and George Ripley, also a Unitarian minister, who was soon to leave the church and found the utopian community of Brook Farm. Most of those who attended the transcendentalist soirees were in their late 20s or early 30s. Thoreau, the youngest, was a welcomed addition. They were a circle of bright, exciting individuals vitally concerned with literature, reform, morality and freedom.

Two people whom Thoreau first encountered at Emerson's home became his close and lifelong friends. Bronson Alcott met Thoreau there in 1839. The following year he moved to Concord and their friendship quickly deepened. An impractical idealist, Alcott was a great talker and possessed a most sunny disposition. Along with Emerson, he was one of the first to recognize Thoreau's genius and potential.

Ellery Channing, like Thoreau, was an aspiring young poet attracted to the Emersonian aura. He first met Thoreau in 1840, though they didn't become close friends until Channing moved to Concord in 1843. Cheerful, witty, much given to flowery speech, and not above telling a risque story now and then, Channing was quite different from Thoreau. Yet the two became fast friends, and from the Walden years until Thoreau's death were almost constant companions, sharing a love of nature and learning. Channing would be Thoreau's first biographer.

A final significant friend Thoreau made at this time was the novelist Nathaniel Hawthorne who, with his wife, Sophia Peabody (Elizabeth's sister), came to live in a large Concord house known as the Old Manse in July, 1842. When the Hawthornes moved in, Emerson suggested to Thoreau that he help them put their garden in order. Henry did so and quickly these two writers took a liking to one another. Soon after that first meeting Hawthorne described Henry in his notebook as

> a singular character; a young man with much of wild, original Nature still remaining in him; and so far as he is sophisticated, it is in a way and method of his own . . . He is a keen and delicate observer of Nature . . . a *genuine* observer, which I suspect is almost as rare a character as

even an original poet. And Nature, in return for his love, seems to adopt him as her especial child; and shows him secrets which few others are allowed to witness.

Hawthorne's daughter Rose, who claimed that her father liked Thoreau best of all men in Concord, once described a skating party:

> One afternoon, Mr. Emerson and Mr. Thoreau went with him [Hawthorne] down the river. Henry Thoreau is an experienced skater, and was figuring dithyrambic [wildly enthusiastic] dances and Bacchic leaps on the ice—very remarkable, but very ugly, methought. Next him followed Mr. Hawthorne who, wrapped in his cloak,moved like a self-impelled Greek statue, stately and grave. Mr. Emerson closed the line, evidently too weary to hold himself erect, pitching head foremost, half lying on the air.

In addition to giving Thoreau a brilliant circle of friends, being part of Emerson's transcendental coterie also encouraged him to develop his abilities as a writer and provided his first opportunities to publish. In 1840, the American transcendentalists started their own journal, the *Dial*.

At first edited by Margaret Fuller and later by Emerson, the *Dial* was launched with great expectations. It was to give voice to a new American literature and to proclaim transcendental truths to a skeptical public. Hopes unfortunately outran realities. The essays, poetry, translations, and reviews that made up a typical edition of the magazine ranged from the near sublime to the utterly ridiculous. The *Dial* never reached a large audience, and in 1844 ceased publication.

Nevertheless, in its four-year existence this journal served the important function of helping young writers to master their craft. This was particularly true for Thoreau. When the first issue was published in July, 1840, it contained one of his poems and one of his essays. All told, 31 of his contributions would be published during the lifespan of the magazine. Reading these early pieces one can see Thoreau finding his voice. Some of his *Dial* essays such as "The Natural History of Massachusetts" and "A Winter Walk" are beautifully written and foreshadow the themes of alienation from society and rapport with nature so central to his later writing.

Working on the *Dial* also gave him editing experience. When Emerson took over the editorship from Fuller, Thoreau assisted him in evaluating and revising manuscripts. In Emerson's absence Thoreau was the sole editor of the April, 1843, issue. This was valuable training for an aspiring author and taught him a great deal about practical aspects of writing and publishing.

Thoreau also worked on his style and ideas by lecturing at the Concord Lyceum. The lyceum movement was a pioneer attempt at adult education and played a vital role in the development of American culture. Beginning with a pamphlet published by Josiah Holbrook in 1826, advocating the creation of lyceums to "raise the moral and intellectual taste of our countrymen," the movement spread rapidly. By the mid-1830s there were more than 3,000 of these associations throughout the country. They sponsored lectures and debates, organized classes, maintained libraries, and in many instances created museums. A typical lyceum over the year would present lectures on literature, science, history, philosophy, music, and current events, as well as humorous talks and travelogues. Emerson, who frequently traveled about the country giving lectures, referred to the lyceum as a "pulpit that makes all other pulpits ineffectual."

Concord opened its own very popular lyceum in 1829. On April 11, 1838, Thoreau delivered his first public lecture there. Throughout the remainder of his life he made many lyceum appearances, often using this platform to develop his Journal writings into more polished, publishable pieces. He frequently served as the lyceum's curator, helping to line up speakers such as Emerson, Alcott, and Brownson. Though Thoreau lectured without charge at Concord, his success there would soon win him invitations to speak at other lyceums for a fee.

Writing for the *Dial* and lecturing at the lyceum were valuable experiences, but they didn't pay the bills. When in the spring of 1841, John's poor health forced the Thoreau brothers to close their school, Henry was once again faced with the problem of how to sustain himself. Fortunately his friend, Emerson, invited him to live at his house. In return for room and board, Henry served as handyman, companion, and babysitter. It proved a good arrangement. Their friendship deepened; Thoreau became even more a part of the intellectual ferment surrounding Emerson; and he developed an affectionate sisterly relationship with Emerson's wife, Lydia.

Though happy at the Emersons', Thoreau dreamed of a place of his own, close to nature. On Christmas Eve, 1841, he wrote in his Journal, "I want to go soon and live away by the pond, where I shall hear only the wind whispering among the reeds. It will be success if I shall have left myself behind. But my friends ask what I will do when I get there. Will it not be employment enough to watch the progress of the seasons?" Early in the new year he remarked similarly, "Why should not Nature revel sometimes, and genially relax and make herself familiar at my board? I would have my house a bower fit to entertain her."

Such reveries were quickly shattered as tragedy struck both the Thoreaus and Emersons in January, 1842. On New Year's Day, Henry's brother, John, cut his finger while sharpening his razor. Tetanus set in and on January 11 John died of lockjaw in his brother's arms. Henry dearly loved his older brother and was ill prepared for his death. On January 22 he had an emotional reaction and came down with all the symptoms of lockjaw himself. He soon recovered, but on the 27th, Emerson's five-year-old son, Waldo, died suddenly of scarlet fever.

So intense was Thoreau's grief that when he could finally bring himself to write in his Journal, more than five weeks after his brother's demise, he simply stated: "I feel as if years had been crowded into the last month." But slowly he came to accept the idea that death was part of the cycle of life. By early March he was able to write of death as "a law and not an accident—It is as common as life." And a few days later: "When we look over the fields we are not saddened because the particular flowers or grasses will wither—for the law of their death is the law of new life . . . So it is with the human plant."

Thoreau's gradual acceptance of death reconfirmed his commitment to probe life's experiences and nature through his writing. But he began to think that perhaps Concord was too confining and that to become a great writer he might have to broaden his horizons. Again Emerson came to his aid. He secured Thoreau a position as tutor in the household of his older brother, William, who lived on Staten Island. The idea was that Thoreau would be able to make contact with the larger literary world of New York City.

Unfortunately, Henry hated New York, describing it in a letter to Emerson as "a thousand times meaner than I could have imagined. It will be something to hate,—that's the advantage it will be to me . . . The pigs in the street are the most respectable part of the population." Though Thoreau did try to sell his various writings to New York editors, the effort was largely in vain. "My bait will not tempt the rats; they are too well fed," he wrote his mother. To Emerson he confessed, "literature comes to a poor market here; and even the little that I write is more than will sell."

But while Thoreau failed to become a New York literary lion, his months there were not entirely wasted. He met some well-known people. Thoreau thought very little of some celebrities. Albert Brisbane, for instance, then famous as the leading American exponent of Fourier socialism,[1] appeared to Thoreau "like a man who has lived in a cellar." On the other hand, Henry James Sr., the father of William, the philosopher, and Henry, the novelist, was to Thoreau "a refreshing forward-looking and forward-moving man." More important for Thoreau's future was his meeting Horace Greeley. Just six years Thoreau's senior, Greeley was already the successful editor of the *New York Tribune*. The two became lifelong friends and in later years Greeley would do everything in his power to sell and promote Thoreau's writings.

While such personal contacts were valuable, Henry found himself homesick for Concord. He wrote to his mother in early August, 1843, thanking her for news of home and family, and telling her, "Methinks I should be content to sit at the back-door in Concord, under the poplar-tree, henceforth forever." He came home that Thanksgiving, then returned to Staten Island only long enough to close his affairs there. December found him back in Concord, this time to stay.

Though his dreams of earning a literary living had been dashed in New York, his determination to be a great writer was

---

[1]Borrowing from the social theories of the Frenchman Charles Fourier, Brisbane advocated the creation of utopian communities in which work would be divided among people according to their natural inclinations. During the 1840s several hundred of these communities were founded in various parts of the country and were being touted as an alternative to capitalism. Brook Farm was for a time Fourierist. By the 1850s the movement was in decline.

stronger than ever. But he still faced the dilemma of how to earn his keep without sacrificing the hours necessary for contemplation and writing. For the time being he moved back in with his parents and helped his father in the pencil-making business. The following year, 1844, he also assisted his father in building a new family home.

Thoreau also made time for frequent excursions in the country. One such trip ended in disaster. On April 30, 1844, Thoreau had set off with a young Harvard student, Edward Hoar, on a boating trip up the Sudbury River. They caught some fish and stopped on the shores of Fair Haven Bay to cook them for lunch. It had been an exceptionally dry spring and their fire quickly spread out of control. Before sufficient help could be summoned to extinguish the blaze some 300 acres of Concord woods and fields burned.

The townspeople were furious and only the fact that Edward Hoar's father was Concord's most prominent citizen seems to have saved the two picnickers from prosecution. Already regarded by many of his fellow citizens as an eccentric loafer who could not hold a regular job, Thoreau's reputation hit a new low. The nature lover had become the woods burner.

Thoreau was despondent. Not only were people making nasty remarks about him, but even his writing career seemed to be going nowhere. The *Dial*, the one journal in which he had published regularly, suspended publication the same month as the fire. His fortunes at their lowest ebb, Thoreau more than ever desired to change his life. He needed solitude to write and a simple enough existence to make earning a living less than a full-time task. His opportunity was not long in coming.

In October, 1844, Emerson bought some 14 acres of land along the shores of Walden Pond. In the winter of 1845, Thoreau received a letter from Channing urging him to go out to Walden, "build yourself a hut, and there begin the grand process of devouring yourself alive." Thoreau, who had long contemplated such a scheme, needed little encouragement. That March, with Emerson's permission and Alcott's axe, he began construction of his pondside cabin. His life was about to take a new course.

4

ECONOMY

A man is rich in proportion to the number
of things he can afford to let alone.
—*Walden*

In some respects Thoreau's first 27 years leading up to Walden might seem uneventful—a happy, small town boyhood; attending a famous, but still rather provincial, college; and his early efforts to establish himself as a writer. Yet in a larger context, the years from Henry's birth in 1817 to his move to Walden in 1845 witnessed the most momentous changes in American history. During this period the United States was transformed from a traditional, agrarian society that was slow to accept innovations, to a modern capitalist industrialized state accustomed to change. Revolutions in transportation, communication and industry characterized this new era, as did the rapid growth of cities and the equally fast settlement of the West. In short, this was the first period of America's modernization.

For some people the advent of this new America was symbolized by specific technological triumphs. For instance, the famous 19th-century intellectual, Henry Adams, who was born in 1838, looked back upon the early years of his childhood as a historic turning point more significant than "had ever happened before in human experience." For him

the old universe was thrown into the ash heap and a new one created. He [Henry Adams] and his eighteenth-century . . . Boston were suddenly cut apart—separated forever—in act if not in sentiment, by the opening of the Boston and Albany Railroad; the appearance of the first Cunard Steamers in the bay; and the telegraphic messages

34

which carried from Baltimore to Washington the news that Henry Clay and James K. Polk were nominated for the Presidency. This was May, 1844; . . . his new world was ready for use, and only fragments of the old met his eyes.

Concord as it appeared a few years before the coming of the railroad. This view is from the steps of the Thoreau home on the Square and shows the First Parish Church where Thoreau was baptized and where his funeral was held. (Author's collection)

Thoreau's 18th-century Concord also symbolically ended about that same time. In June, 1844, the first train arrived in town. This was part of a railroad that ran from Boston to Fitchburg. Built largely by Irish laborers working as long as 16 hours a day for a daily wage of only $.60, the new train replaced the uncomfortable stagecoach and reduced the travel time it took to go from Concord to Boston from four hours to less than an hour. The railroad made Concord much more part of the outside world, not just of Boston, but of an expanding, dynamic, national economy. Local farmers lost a great deal of their earlier independence as they came to rely on the railroad to sell their crops in the cities. Industry and commerce also expanded in the town.

The new railroad ravaged the natural world of Walden. The tracks passed so close to the west side of the pond that one cove had to be filled in to accommodate the high embankment on which the rails were laid. This cut in the earth was visible from Thoreau's cabin. Henry was not pleased by the railroad's violation of nature. "That devilish Iron Horse," he wrote in

Walden, "whose ear-rending neigh is heard throughout the town, has muddied the Boiling Spring with his foot, and he it is that has browsed off all the woods on Walden shore, that Trojan horse, with a thousand men in his belly, introduced by mercenary Greeks! Where is the country's champion . . . to meet him at the Deep Cut and thrust an avenging lance between the ribs of the bloated pest?"

The railroad was not all that bothered Thoreau. This "devilish Iron Horse" was only the most obvious sign of more sweeping changes affecting not just Concord, but the whole nation. As the new world of industrial capitalism spread, old moral values and small town mores gave way to a more acquisitive spirit. Thoreau was appalled by his townsmen's absorption in business and money-making. He felt such pursuits had become ends in themselves and thus distorted the real purpose of living. "This world is a place of business," he lamented.

> What an infinite bustle! I am awakened almost every night by the panting of the locomotive. It interrupts my dreams. There is no sabbath. It would be glorious to see mankind at leisure for once. It is nothing but work, work, work. I cannot easily buy a blank book to write thoughts in; they are commonly ruled for dollars and cents . . . If a man is tossed out a window when an infant, or scared out of his wits by the Indians, it is regretted chiefly because he was thus incapacitated for business! I think there is nothing, not even crime, more opposed to poetry, to philosophy, ay to life itself, than this incessant business.

Thoreau was not alone in attacking what he termed "the curse of trade." Indeed the whole transcendental movement of which he was a part can be seen as a reaction to America's excessive materialism, and several of his transcendentalist friends tried to offer the country alternatives to capitalism. Orestes Brownson, in a series of essays published in the early 1840s attacked the factory labor system then spreading throughout New England. "Wages," he wrote, "is a cunning device of the devil for the benefit of tender consciences who would retain all the advantages of the slave system without the expense, trouble, and odium of being slaveholders."

In the spring of 1843, Thoreau's close friend, Bronson Alcott, founded a short-lived utopian community called Fruitlands which he had hoped would be a second Eden, a community that would "restore Man to his rightful communion with God in the Paradise of Good."

By far the most famous transcendental experiment in communal living was Brook Farm. Founded by Emerson's cousin George Ripley, in the spring of 1841, Brook Farm was located some 12 miles to the southeast of Thoreau's Walden, in an idyllic setting of gently rolling hills, green meadows, and tall pines. The aim of this experimental community was, according to Ripley,

> to insure a more natural union between intellectual and manual labor than now exists; to combine the thinker and the worker, as far as possible, in the same individual; to guarantee the highest mental freedom, by providing all with labor, adapted to their tastes and talents, and securing to them the fruits of their industry; to do away [with] the necessity of menial services, by opening the benefits of education and the profits of labor to all; and thus to prepare a society of liberal, intelligent, and cultivated persons, whose relations with each other would permit a more simple and wholesome life, than can be led amidst the pressure of our competitive institutions.

Until a disastrous fire brought an end to Brook Farm in 1847, it was an exciting, happy adventure in living and reform.

Both Alcott and Ripley had asked Thoreau to join their respective communities. But while he sympathized with their goals, he was too much of an individualist to participate in any of the utopian communes of his age. To Ripley he remarked: "As for these communities, I think I had rather keep bachelor's hall in hell than go board in heaven." Emerson also declined to enlist, telling his cousin that "all I shall solidly do, I must do alone."

Yet while Thoreau was clearly more individualistic than Alcott and Ripley, his Walden experiment was as much an attempt at reform as were the Fruitlands and Brook Farm communities. When Thoreau moved to the woods on Independence Day in 1845, his hope was to lay a new foundation for American liberty, to create an alternative to materialistic capitalism.

Henry Thoreau was certainly not the first young man to go off to live alone in the wilds. Thousands of Americans annually trekked off to the western frontier, some to dwell in places so remote they would make Walden appear absolutely tame by comparison. Nor was Thoreau even the first intellectual to seek the solitude of nature for purposes of contemplation and writing. Thoreau's close friend, Ellery Channing, had lived for a time alone in a hut on the Illinois prairies. Stearns Wheeler, a Harvard classmate, had built a cabin on the shores of Flint's Pond in nearby Lincoln, where Thoreau spent six pleasant weeks during the summer of 1837.

Yet, if Thoreau cannot be credited with being the first of his contemporaries to go off to live alone, he was the first to write about his life in the woods as a challenge to the dominant American values. He was a reformer with a message. The first and longest chapter of *Walden* is entitled "Economy." It is an indictment of what he saw as the "lives of quiet desperation" led by the great majority of his contemporaries. Driven by greed and venality, the typical citizen appeared to Thoreau as a "mean and sneaking" individual caught up in the dull routine of joyless money-making.

Wealth became more desirable than the pursuit of life's highest goals, and earning a living seemed more important than living itself. Thoreau saw most work as a kind of enslavement. "There are so many keen and subtle masters that enslave both North and South. It is hard to have a Southern overseer; it is worse to have a Northern one; but worst of all when you are the slave-driver of yourself." He felt people had lost their free will. They dressed according to the dictates of fashion; they unthinkingly accepted the standards of their peers whether it suited their lives or not; and they filled their houses with costly, pretentious furnishings. According to Thoreau, Americans adopted the customary modes of living not out of preference, but because they "honestly think there is no choice left." This was nonsense. "There are as many ways" to live, he insisted, as "can be drawn radii from one centre."

Thoreau believed that his contemporaries, in their haste to "progress," had lost their sense of values: "If a man walks in the woods for love of them half of each day, he is in danger of being regarded as a loafer; but if he spends his whole day as a speculator, shearing off those woods and making the earth bald before her time, he is esteemed as an industrious and enterprising citizen. As if a town had no interest in its forest but to cut them down!" The exploitation of nature about which he complained was *progress* to most Americans. Cutting down trees cleared land for farming and made money in lumber as well. Money bought more and fancier possessions. Henry thanked God that at least "man as yet cannot fly, and lay waste the sky as well as the earth."

Thoreau believed that "men labor under a mistake. The better part of the man is soon plowed into the soil for compost." As for possessions, he had seen too many of his townsmen "whose misfortune it is to have inherited farms, houses, barns, cattle, and farming tools." These were "inherited encumbrances," that enslaved people rather than liberated them. Possessions created needless cares and bound people to the "superfluously coarse labors of life," stealing their leisure and robbing them of the "finer fruits" of existence. "How many a poor immortal soul have I met well-nigh crushed and smothered under its load, creeping down the road of life, pushing before it a barn seventy-five feet by forty, . . . and one hundred acres of land, tillage, mowing, pasture, and wood-lot!"

Most labor, Thoreau felt, was of little more value than "throwing stones over a wall and then . . . throwing them back again." He particularly questioned the technological improvements of the age:

> The nation itself, with all its so-called internal improvements, which by the way, are all external and superficial, is just such an unwieldly and overgrown establishment, cluttered with furniture and tripped up by its own traps, ruined by luxury, and heedless expense, by want of calculation and a worthy aim . . . It lives too fast. Men think that it is essential that the Nation have commerce, and export ice, and talk through a telegraph, and ride thirty miles an hour . . . but whether we live like baboons or like men, is a little uncertain.

Many of Thoreau's criticisms of American society were directed against technology. It was not so much the machine he distrusted but the uses to which it was put. As a skilled carpenter and surveyor, Thoreau admired useful machines. In fact, while helping his father in the pencil-making business he invented a new grinding mill for graphite, a saw to cut out individual leads, and a machine to drill a hole in the wood for the lead, rather than cutting the wood in half and then gluing it back together. These ingenious devices, along with his innovative formula for mixing the lead, helped his father produce the finest pencils made in America at that time. Clearly Thoreau's understanding and appreciation of machinery made his criticism of mechanization an earned opinion.

Ideally, machinery should serve to reduce human labor and thereby free people for higher pursuits. But as Thoreau realized, this was not the case in practice. Instead of machinery serving human needs, people served the needs of the machine: "men have become the tools of their tools." Rather than being a liberating force, machinery had become an instrument of oppression. "We do not ride upon the railroad; it rides upon us."

In Thoreau's view it was the common laborer who suffered most drastically from the new reliance on machine power. With the advent of the factory system work was increasingly subdivided and mechanized. Under such circumstances, Thoreau observed, "the laboring man has not leisure for a true integrity day by day; he cannot afford to sustain the manliest relations to men; his labor would be depreciated in the market. He has no time to be anything but a machine." Under such a system labor was debased. Workers were dehumanized and alienated from their true selves.

In place of the mechanized productive process with its division of labor, Thoreau sought to restore a wholeness to work. His ideal was the artisan whose labors aspired to perfection without regard for the marketplace. The artisan's work reflected the union of physical and mental effort. He or she would "oversee all the details" of production. And he was " . . . at once pilot and captain, and owner and underwriter."

In the "Conclusion" of *Walden*, Thoreau created the fable of the artist of Kouroo who in striving for perfection in carving a walking stick achieved "elevated piety" and "perennial youth." "The material was pure, and his art was pure; how could the result be other than wonderful?" Such artisans, able to elevate labor into an artistic activity and to find fulfillment of both body and soul in their work, represented an ideal that Thoreau rarely encountered in the Concord of his day.

But he had another model of the exemplary worker as well. This was the independent, self-sufficient farmer. Like Thomas Jefferson, he believed that working the land for one's own necessities brought moral and spiritual rewards as well as economic ones. "Healthily and properly pursued," Thoreau claimed, farming "is not a whit more grave than huckleberrying."

In the 1840s and 1850s there were still a few oldtimers who lived well without regard to the economy of the market. Thoreau particularly praised George Minott, a native of Concord who farmed on the hill opposite Emerson's house. In 1854, Minott confided to Thoreau that the last time he had visited Boston was in 1815. Completely self-reliant, Minott grew his own food, hunted and fished for meat, made maple sugar, and chopped his own firewood. To Thoreau he was "the most poetical farmer—who most realizes to me the poetry of the farmer's life—that I know."

Yet Thoreau realized that George Minott and farmers like him were a rapidly disappearing breed. Most Concord farmers eagerly participated in the market economy and treated fields, woodlots, cattle, and corn as mere investments. Sadly Thoreau pointed out how misguided the farmer was "endeavoring to solve the problem of a livelihood by a formula more complicated than the problem itself. To get his shoestrings he speculates in herds of cattle. With consummate skill he has set his trap with a hair spring to catch comfort and independence, and then, as he turned away, got his own leg into it."

Commercial farming fostered dependence on others and bred servility. Nature for such farmers was mere commodity. In *Walden*, Thoreau described a farmer named Flint "who loved better the reflecting surface of a dollar" than the lovely pond that bore his name. "I respect not his labors," wrote Thoreau of Flint, "his farm where every thing has its price; who would carry the landscape, who would carry his God, to market, if he could get any thing for him; who goes to market *for* his god as it is; on whose farm nothing grows free, whose fields bear no crops, whose meadows no flowers, whose trees no fruits, but dollars; who loves not the beauty of his fruits, whose fruits are not ripe for him till they are turned to dollars."

Farming too had been tainted by the "curse of trade." Farmers had become the "serfs of the soil" who in devoting themselves to "buying and selling" had lost all sense of the higher purpose of life. Agriculture, Thoreau concluded, "was once a sacred art; but it is pursued with irreverent haste and heedlessness by us, our object being to have large farms and large crops merely."

With farming corrupted and most labor debased, how was one to make work meaningful in what Thoreau called "this restless, nervous, bustling, trivial Nineteenth Century?" Henry Thoreau sought an answer in a new mode of life at Walden Pond, and one of his principle purposes in writing *Walden* was to present his findings to the world. In a lecture he delivered to his neighbors at the Concord Lyceum, he noted: "It is remarkable that there is little or nothing to be remembered written on the subject of getting a living; how to make getting a living not merely honest and honorable, but altogether inviting and glorious; for if *getting* a living is not so, then living is not." *Walden*, he hoped, would provide the advice necessary to make such "glorious" living possible.

Since Thoreau believed "trade" to be the root cause of his contemporaries' ills, he tried as much as possible to avoid the economy of the marketplace. At the pond he was able to sit "rapt in a revery, amidst the pines and . . . sumacs, in undisturbed solitude and stillness." His days, unlike those in town, were not "minced into hours and fretted by the ticking of a clock." He had escaped the dominion of the machine. With simple hand tools he built his own house and tended his garden.

Yet even Thoreau could not entirely avoid the marketplace. To achieve economic independence he practiced commercial farming on a small scale. At Walden he raised beans as a cash crop. According to his precise calculations this venture netted him a yearly profit of $8.71½. However, this sum was not enough to meet all his expenses and on occasion he hired himself out as a day laborer.

But despite these compromises with capitalism, Thoreau never accepted full-time work. He felt such a practice would require "sell[ing] both my forenoons and afternoons to society," thereby neglecting his "peculiar calling." To have worked full time would mean "there would be nothing left worth living for."

By simplifying his needs to the barest essentials, he found he was able to support himself quite easily with no more than six weeks of work per year. "I am convinced," he wrote to his friend Horace Greeley, "that to maintain one's self on this earth is not a hardship but a pastime, if we will live simply and wisely . . . It is not necessary that a man should earn his living by the sweat of his brow, unless he sweats easier than I do."

The only cure for America's ills, Thoreau thought, would be "in rigid economy, a stern and more Spartan simplicity of life and elevation of purpose." People worked needlessly long to accumulate extravagant frills: "Most of the luxuries, and many of the so-called comforts of life, are not only not indispensable, but positive hinderances to the elevation of mankind." The truly successful person is not he who "has got much money, many houses and barns and woodlots," but he was has been "trying to better his condition in a higher sense than this, has been trying to invent something, to be somebody,—i.e., to invent and get a patent for himself."

Throughout *Walden* Thoreau exhorts his readers to open "new channels, not of trade, but of thought." Obviously it would have been impossible for all Americas to go off to live in some pondside retreat. This was never Thoreau's advice: "I would not have any one adopt *my* mode of living on any account." What he was advocating was that each individual "be very careful to find out and pursue *his own* way, and not his father's or his mother's or his neighbor's instead."

Having shown the limits of material progress as a goal, Thoreau urged his readers to reevaluate their lives and seek more spiritual ends. "In the long run," he wrote, "men hit only what they aim at. Therefore, though they should fail immediately, they had better aim at something high." He exhorted his neighbors to look beyond the world of material objects: "I perceive that we inhabitants of New England live this mean life that we do because our vision does not penetrate the surface of things." Nature was the key to spiritual perception, but excessive labor did not allow most people to comprehend the spiritual essence of the natural world: "After a hard day's work without a thought, turning my very brain into a mere tool, only in the quiet of evening do I so far recover my senses as to hear the cricket, which in fact has been chirping all day."

Thoreau "heard the cricket" at Walden. There he found an alternative to the bustling, materialistic, expansive, exploitive America of slavery, factories, and economic centralization. Though few of his contemporaries heeded his advice, his example of moral and physical self-sufficiency remains an inspiration to this day.

5

NATURE

Ah, dear nature, the mere remembrance,
after a short forgetfulness, of the pine
woods! I come to it as a hungry man to a
crust of bread.
              —*Journal*, December 12, 1851

Meeting Thoreau in March, 1847, Edwin Whipple, a literary critic, described him as "a man who had experienced Nature as other men are said to have experienced religion." Others were more skeptical. Thoreau's neighbor, Elizabeth Hoar, sarcastically stated: "Henry talks about Nature just as if she's been born and brought up in Concord." But whatever his contemporaries thought, Thoreau's love of nature was an all consuming, lifelong passion. He perpetually craved "a nature which I cannot put my foot through, woods where the wood-thrush for ever sings, where the hours are early morning ones and the day is for ever improved, where I might have a fertile unknown for a soil about me."

Though many Americans today enjoy whatever unspoiled pockets of nature they can find, this has not always been the case. Stepping off the *Mayflower* in 1620, Pilgrim leader William Bradford found "a hideous and desolate wilderness full of wild beasts and wild men." To such 17th-century Puritans the natural world was a place of evil beyond the restraints of civilization. Nature tempted people to sin and thus stood as a barrier between them and their God.

In the 18th century, nature was generally viewed more positively, though chiefly as a field for scientific inquiry rather than inspiration. Intellectuals searched for universal "laws of nature" with little regard for the particular. Their chief symbol of nature was the image of the well-tended garden. They had no aesthetic appreciation for such irregular natural features as mountains or waterfalls.

Asher Durand's painting Kindred Spirits *shows painter Thomas Cole and poet William Cullen Bryant in the Catskills. Such paintings typified the romantic artists' search for the sublime in nature.* (Collection of the New York Public Library, Astor, Lenox and Tilden Foundation)

Not until the more romantic 19th century did large numbers of Americans come to appreciate the beauty of nature. Then, for the first time, the idea of nature as an uplifting force and a respite from the complexities of civilization became important. By the 1830s romantic landscape painters such as Thomas Cole and Asher Durand tried to capture the natural beauty of the American wilderness. "All nature here is new to art," wrote Cole, "primeval forests, virgin lakes, and waterfalls." People became excited about such natural wonders as Niagara Falls, the Hudson River Valley, the Catskills, and the White Mountains. To the romantic mind such sights were wild, exotic, and sublime.

Originating in Europe, the romantic movement came to dominate American culture in the first four decades of the 19th century. Transcendentalism, which emerged in the 1830s, was the most significant philosophical outgrowth of American romanticism. The transcendentalists carried the romantics' appreciation of nature to new heights. For them nature was more than its component physical elements. It was a projection of the divine spirit. Only "aliens from God," claimed Emerson, are "strangers in nature."

Yet while Emerson and other transcendentalists could exhort their countrymen to seek "the Universal Being" in "the flowers, the animals, the mountains," to find "in the wilderness something more dear and connate than in streets or villages," only Thoreau among these New England thinkers was truly at home in nature. Frequently he proclaimed his "inexpressible happiness" in the outdoors, and noted his own "peculiarly wild nature, which so yearns toward all wilderness." Even when not dwelling alone in the woods of Walden, he spent a good part of each day exploring the natural world.

As a young man he developed what became his lifelong habit of taking daily hikes, boat trips or skating excursions. He did this in all seasons, never minding winter snows, spring showers, summer suns or autumn storms. His pattern was to use his mornings and sometimes his evenings for reading and writing, reserving afternoons for his outdoor adventures. He did not walk merely for exercise or amusement. His outings were serious matters. "I go out," he said, "to see what I have caught in my traps which I set for facts." Unlike Emerson, who tended to view nature in the abstract, Thoreau paid close attention to every detail. He invariably carried with him a notebook and pencil to jot down his observations, a spy-glass for taking closer looks at birds and animals, a surveyor's tape to measure such things as the depths of snows or the girth of trees, and an old music book of his father's which he used to press flowers and leaves. An avid collector, he had his tailor make him pants with extra large pockets to accommodate the various nuts, apples, stones, seeds, lichens or other objects that caught his eye. On occasion, he even used his hat to hold specimens of frogs or salamanders he wished to examine more closely.

Thoreau, who stood five feet, seven inches, was of average stature for that time. He had an attractive open face with a broad forehead, a strong Roman nose, and a slightly receding chin that he covered in his last years with a beard. He had a full head of fine light brown hair and a ruddy complexion from spending so much time out-of-doors. But what people noticed most about him were his deep set, piercing blue-gray eyes. Some said he looked like Emerson, though there was no mistaking the two when they walked. Emerson stepped in a deliberate, contemplative way; Thoreau, on the other hand, strided with unusual energy and often covered more than 30 miles in one day.

In addition to his daily outings, he sometimes took longer excursions that involved camping out. His first adventure of this sort was a memorable two-week boat trip on the Concord and Merrimack Rivers he took with his brother, John, in the summer of 1839. In later life he would hike, canoe, and camp in the Maine wilderness, the White Mountains, the Catskills, Canada, and Cape Cod.

Thoreau was an avid mountain climber. One of his favorite peaks was Mount Monadnock, a beautiful isolated mountain in southern New Hampshire that was visible from the hills around Concord. On one of his Monadnock adventures he was accompanied by Ellery Channing, his friend and most frequent hiking companion. Taking a train to Troy, New Hampshire they immediately shouldered their packs and set out for the mountain. Thoreau's and Channing's technique on such climbs was to take a compass bearing of the peak from their starting point and then to set off in a straight line through fields, forests, swamps, and brooks with no deviation in their course. According to one account, they once found a farmhouse in their line of walk but simply marched through the front door and out the back to the astonishment of the family sitting at their dining table. Once they got to the mountain, Channing claimed, Thoreau "would run up the steepest place as swiftly as if he were on smooth land, and his breath never failed."

On this particular outing they reached the summit about 3:00 P.M. A heavy rain was falling. Finding a sheltered spot to camp, Thoreau took his hatchet and set about building a quite substantial lean-to with a water-tight roof thatched with spruce branches. Channing declared the hut "the handsomest he ever saw." It was about dark before the shelter was finished, and by that time, according to Thoreau's later account, "we were nearly as wet as if we had stood in a hogshead of water. We then built a fire before the door . . . Standing before this, and turning round slowly, like meat that is roasting, we were as dry if not drier than ever after a few hours." Soon the weather cleared and they could see the stars and hear the singing of the nighthawks.

During the five days they spent on the mountain the two campers would go to the summit each evening to watch the sunset. Thoreau was elated to find "an elysium beneath me. The smoky haze of the day, suggesting a furnace-like heat, a trivial dustiness, gave place to a clear transparent enamel, through which houses, woods, farms, and lakes were seen as in a picture indescribably fair and expressly made to be looked at."

Their days were spent observing the mountain's flora and fauna. Thoreau filled his notebook with detailed data on flowers, birds, lichens, and rocks. They explored the various spurs of the mountain and with the help of his compass Thoreau made a map of the area.

Thoreau especially cherished these expeditions because they brought him into wilder realms than his native Concord could offer. He was always glad to "discover, in oceans and wilderness far away, the materials out of which a million Concords can be made—indeed unless I discover them, I am lost myself." In addressing his townspeople assembled before the Concord Lyceum on April 23, 1851, he elaborated on this: "I wish to speak a word for Nature, for absolute freedom and wildness, as contrasted with a freedom and culture merely civil." Continuing in this vein he declared: "Let me live where I will, on this side is the city, on that the wilderness, and ever I am leaving the city more and more, and withdrawing into the wilderness." He concluded with the simple assertion that "in Wildness is the preservation of the World."

This bold statement was basic to Thoreau's, and later America's, conservation ethic. True civilization, he believed, could not exist in the absence of wilderness. The real energy of a nation came from the wild. "The story of Romulus and Remus being suckled by a wolf is not a meaningless fable," he argued. "The founders of every state which has risen to eminence have drawn their nourishment and vigor from a similar wild source." In his lyceum talk he claimed that "the forest and wilderness" furnished "the tonics and barks which brace mankind." Even in literature, he affirmed, "it is only the wild that attracts us." Classics such as the *Iliad*, *Hamlet*, or even the Bible appealed to us, he maintained, because they were "as wildly natural and primitive, mysterious and marvelous, ambrosial and fertile, as a fungus or a lichen." "Life consists with wildness. The most alive is the wildest."

This love of wildness led Thoreau to celebrate the frontier West. "We go eastward to realize history . . . we go westward as into the future." Having a vast frontier, what Thoreau referred to as "being flanked by the Fur Countries," made America superior to Europe. "I must walk toward Oregon, and not toward Europe. And that way the nation is moving, and I may say that mankind progress from east to west." In this country people lived life closer to wilderness, to the "raw-material of life." He wrote "that Adam in paradise was not so favorably situated on the whole as is the backwoodsman in America." Wilderness, he believed, was the best place in which to "settle ourselves, and work and wedge our feet downward through the mud and slush of opinion, and prejudice, and tradition, and delusion . . . through Paris and London, through New York and Boston . . . till we come to hard bottom and rocks in place, which we call *reality*."

Many of Thoreau's contemporaries, including even some of his transcendentalist friends, mistrusted Henry's call of the wild. Emerson, for instance, wrote that while the "first steps from the town to the woods" were "very seductive," "the end is want and madness." Charles Lane, another transcendentalist, described the "free life in the woods" as "savage, barbarous, and brutal," and contrasted this with the "refined, polished, and elevated . . . life" of civilization.

But Thoreau was not advocating a crude primitivism. Though he greatly admired the American Indian and could speak affectionately of "the wild savage in us," wilderness for him was highly moral. To uncover and understand the wild within us was to attain perfect freedom. In seeking wilderness, Thoreau wrote, "we saunter toward the Holy Land, till one day the sun shall shine more brightly than ever he has done, shall perchance shine into our minds and hearts, and light up our whole lives with a great awakening light, as warm and serene and golden as on a bankside in autumn."

Wilderness was not an end in itself, nor a desired permanent habitat. Rather it was a place of purification and renewal. Withdrawing from society to nature allowed one to see more clearly the possibilities and principles of a new life. Thoreau had no desire to live forever apart from civilization. Indeed, after two weeks in the primitive wilds of the Maine woods he wrote: "It was a relief to get back to our smooth, but still varied landscape. For a permanent residence, it seemed to me there could be no comparison between this and the wilderness, necessary as the latter is for a resource and a background, the raw material of all our civilization."

His ultimate goal was to join the primitive virtues of the wild with the highest values of civilization, to unite the best of country and city, to be, as he described his bean field, "half-cultivated." In writing about his life at Walden he remarked how much he enjoyed "the retirement and solitude of an early settler." But he went on to say "and yet there may be a lyceum in the evening and there is a book-shop and library in the village, and five times a day I can be whirled to Boston within an hour." Despite his isolation at the pond, Thoreau led a remarkably civilized life. He read Homer and Cicero, wrote two books and had a rich social life.

But without nature, Thoreau believed, civilization would close in on itself and ultimately perish. "We can never have enough of Nature. We must be refreshed by the sight of inexhaustible vigor, vast and Titanic features, the sea-coast with its wrecks, the wilderness with its living and its decaying trees, the thundercloud, and the rain which lasts three weeks and produce freshets. We need to witness our own limits transgressed, and some life pasturing freely where we never wander."

Thoreau recommended the creation of "national preserves" of wilderness. This was not inspired by hostility to human society, but by the belief that true civilization required periodic infusions of the spirit of wildness. "Each town," he wrote, "should have a park, or rather a primitive forest, of five hundred or a thousand acres, where a stick should never be cut for fuel, a common possession forever, for instruction and recreation. We hear of cow-commons and ministerial lots, but we want *men*-commons and lay lots, inalienable forever."

This philosophy anticipated the present day conservationist ethic. Most of Thoreau's contemporaries assumed the earth's resources to be endless and looked upon the natural environment as existing to serve society's material needs. Thoreau was appalled by this attitude: "If some are persecuted for abusing children, others deserve to be prosecuted for maltreating the face of nature committed to their care." He was particularly upset by the destruction of the forest.

> Strange that so few ever come to the woods to see how the pine tree lives and grows and spires, lifting its evergreen arms to the light—to see its perfect success; but most are content to behold it in the shape of many broad boards brought to market, and deem *that* its true success! But the pine is no more lumber than man is, and to be made into boards and houses is no more its true and highest use than the truest use of a man is to be cut down and made into manure. There is a higher law affecting our relation to pines as well as to men . . . Every creature is better alive than dead, men and moose and pine trees, and he who understands it aright will rather preserve its life than destroy it.

In this context, Thoreau was much more than a pioneer conservationist. Although the word was not yet coined in his day, he was what is known today as an ecologist. He believed in the interdependency of all living things. To cut the forests and hunt species of birds or animals to extinction was to do irreparable harm to the earth. "What is the use of a house," he once asked a friend, "if you haven't got a tolerable planet to put it on?" The earth to Thoreau was "not a mere fragment of dead history, stratum upon stratum like the leaves of a book, to be studied by geologists and antiquaries chiefly, but living poetry like the leaves of a tree, which precede flowers and fruit,—not a fossil earth, but a living earth; compared with whose great central life all animal and vegetable life is merely parasitic." To preserve the earth's health, Thoreau argued, one had to respect all living things and to recognize the delicate balance of nature in which all life was organically connected.

He tried to teach his own and succeeding generations the necessity of living within the absolute laws of nature, of not tampering with this intricate, organic universe. Why, he chided, "improve and beautify the system? What to make the stars shine more brightly, the sun more cheery and joyous, the moon more placid and content." Rather than cut the forest, he urged, "can we not assist in its interior economy, in the circulation of the sap?"

Thoreau's passion for nature was intense and uncompromising. Nature served many purposes for him. It was a source of health—spiritual as well as physical. "You must converse much with the field and woods," he wrote, "if you would imbibe such health into your mind and spirit as you covet for your body." Nature was life affirming. It rejuvenated the human spirit. "In society you will not find health," he claimed. "Society is always diseased, and the best is most so. There is no scent in it so wholesome as that of the pines, nor any fragrance so penetrating as the life-everlasting in high pastures."

Nature also allowed people to escape the confines of history. People brought up in society lived by the authority of the past. History was perceived as linear. Nations, like people, went from youth to age to ultimate death. Each generation seemed bound by the institutions and values of those generations preceding them. Nature, Thoreau believed, offered a way to elude such historic determinism. History for him was but the surface of human experience. Nature, although far older and deeper than history, was, nevertheless, forever young. Instead of following a straight path to death, nature followed the cycles of the seasons and was always being reborn. To choose nature over history, therefore, was to choose personal freedom and a world of inexhaustible possibilities.

This idea of the endless renewal of the seasons comforted Thoreau following the death of his beloved brother, John, in 1842. Soon after this tragedy he wrote, "how plain that death is only the phenomenon of the individual . . . Nature does not recognize it, she finds her own again under new forms." He asserted that death was "a law and not an accident—It is as common as life. When we look over the fields we are not saddened because the particular flowers or grasses will wither—for the law of their death is the law of new life . . . So it is with the human plant." Nature, he came to realize, must sacrifice life to advance life. Nature was "so rife with life that myriads can be afforded to be sacrificed."

Above all, nature served Thoreau as the source of spiritual and artistic inspiration. As a transcendental idealist he believed that natural objects, if rightly seen, reflected universal spiritual truths. "Let us not underrate the value of a fact," he affirmed; "it will one day flower in a truth." Nature was the proper source of religion. "These motions everywhere in nature," he observed, "must surely [be] the circulations of God. The flowing sail, the running stream, the waving tree, the roving wind,—whence else their infinite health and freedom?" Thoreau tried to capture the moral and spiritual meaning of nature in his prose. Walking in the snow with the sun behind him on a bright, cold winter day he saw his shadow in front of him, not black, but "a most celestial blue."

His quest for the spiritual truth of nature was not always fulfilled. In a lovely passage in *Walden* he writes: "I long ago lost a hound, a bay horse, and a turtle-dove, and am still on their trail. Many are the travellers I have spoken concerning them, describing their tracks and what calls they answered to. I have met one or two who had heard the hound, and the tramp of the horse, and even seen the dove disappear behind a cloud, and they seemed as anxious to recover them as if they had lost them themselves." The symbolic hound, horse, and dove represented the spiritual reality behind nature. He spent his life in their pursuit. In recording this he left us a most intimate and beautiful portrait of a man's interaction with the natural world.

6

TWO BOOKS

If a man does not keep pace with his companions, perhaps it is because he hears a different drummer. Let him step to the music which he hears, however measured or far away.

—*Walden*

Henry Thoreau's move to Walden pond in the summer of 1845 was a deliberate effort to mold himself into the transcendental hero, to follow his "different drummer" and listen to the dictates of nature and not of society. He wished to be the poet-hero, to write a sentence that "should read as if its author, had he held a plow instead of a pen, could have drawn a furrow deep and straight to the end." Soon after settling in at Walden he began writing what would become his first published book, *A Week on the Concord and Merrimack Rivers*. With a surge of creative energy he finished a first draft of the book by fall, and a second, expanded draft, by spring of 1846.

The inspiration for the book was the boating and hiking trip Thoreau had taken with his brother, John, in 1839. That spring the brothers had built a 15-foot fisherman's dory which they had ingeniously fitted with wheels so that they could easily portage it around falls and other obstacles. The boat was also equipped with two sets of oars, several slender poles for shoving in shallow places and two sailing masts, one of which served as their tent pole at night. On Saturday, August 31st, they set out: "we two, brothers, and natives of Concord, weighed anchor in this river port." They carried melons and potatoes from their garden for food, a cotton canvas cloth for a tent, and buffalo skins for their beds.

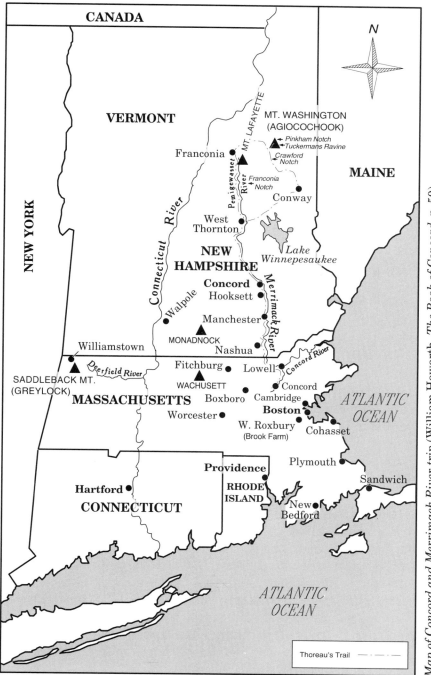

CANADA

VERMONT

MT. WASHINGTON
(AGIOCOCHOOK)

Pinkham Notch
Tuckermans Ravine

Crawford
Notch

Franconia

MAINE

Franconia
Notch

Conway

NEW YORK

Connecticut River

Pemigewasset River

MT. LAFAYETTE

West
Thornton

NEW
HAMPSHIRE

Lake
Winnepesaukee

Concord
Hooksett

Merrimack River

Walpole

Manchester

MONADNOCK

Williamstown

Nashua

SADDLEBACK MT.
(GREYLOCK)

Deerfield River

Fitchburg

WACHUSETT

Lowell

Concord River

Concord

MASSACHUSETTS

Boxboro

Cambridge

ATLANTIC
OCEAN

Worcester

Boston

W. Roxbury
(Brook Farm)

Cohasset

Plymouth

Providence

Sandwich

Hartford

RHODE
ISLAND

CONNECTICUT

New
Bedford

ATLANTIC
OCEAN

Thoreau's Trail

Map of Concord and Merrimack River trip (William Howarth, The Book of Concord, p. 50)

The trip was idyllic. For five days they rowed and sailed down the Concord River and then up the Merrimack, camping at lovely spots along the way. Though their voyage took them past the bustling mill towns of Lowell, Massachusetts and Nashua and Manchester, New Hampshire, it was nature they observed. Arriving at Hooksett, New Hampshire on Wednesday evening, they stored their boat with an obliging farmer. After a stage ride to Plymouth, New Hampshire the following morning, they spent the next several days hiking in the White Mountains, including a climb to the top of Mount Washington, the highest peak in the range. Retracing their route, they returned to Hooksett on Thursday, September 12. The next day, with favorable winds and currents most of the way, they had an exhilarating sail and row the whole 50 miles back to Concord.

Thoreau kept a journal during the trip and had begun to conceive of an essay on this excursion as early as 1840. Only after John's death in 1842 did the idea occur to him to write a book about the expedition as a memorial to his brother. However other activities delayed his work on this project. He needed to escape his busy schedule and devote more time toward finishing the book. To some degree then, Henry's decision to go to Walden was inspired by his desire to write *A Week*.

The rapid completion of the book at Walden elated him. He read parts of it to Bronson Alcott who praised it as "purely American, fragrant with the lives of New England woods and streams." Emerson, too, was impressed and tried to secure a publisher. On July 16, 1846, he wrote to a friend "in a short time, if Wiley & Putnam smile, you shall have Henry Thoreau's 'Excursion on Concord & Merrimack Rivers,' a seven days' voyage in as many chapters."

But Wiley and Putnam did not "smile," nor were other publishers particularly interested, though most were willing to print the book at Thoreau's expense. Annoyed at this, Henry withdrew the manuscript and made further revisions. Finally, in 1848, the Boston publisher James Munroe & Co. agreed to publish *A Week*, providing that Thoreau guaranteed their costs. They also promised to release Thoreau's second book, *Walden*, which he had also completed at the pond. Although reluctant because of the financial arrangements he, nevertheless, agreed, and on May 30, 1849, *A Week on the Concord and Merrimack Rivers* was published.

Most of the reviews were favorable. *Holden's Dollar Magazine* called *A Week* "a rare work in American literature," and advised their "readers to procure it. It is full of fine thoughts and pleasant descriptions of nature." A writer for the *New Hampshire Patriot* praised it as "a remarkable volume and its author a remarkable man . . . The author . . . is a man of thought—retired from the busy scenes of life, he turns the mental eye inward and endeavors to read the mysterious page of his own soul . . . On closing the book we find ourselves in love with the author, satisfied with ourselves and at peace with the world."

Even in England, where American books were frequently scorned, Sophia Dobson Collet wrote in the London *People's Review*: "The writer describes the scenery of his voyage with the vividness of a painter, and the scrutiny of a naturalist . . . Every object seen is, with him, an element in a higher vision . . . The occasional digressions are . . . not unworthy to stand beside [the essays] of Emerson himself."

But the reviews were not all good. Two things in particular disturbed some readers. First, they were bothered by what one reviewer called Thoreau's "Pantheistic egoism" and unchristian outlook. Passages such as: "It is necessary not to be Christian to appreciate the beauty and significance of the life of Christ," were offensive to Christian readers.

The second problem concerned digressions. Poet and critic James Russell Lowell complained in the *Massachusetts Quarterly Review*: "We come upon them [digressions] like snags jolting us head foremost out of our places as we are rowing placidly up stream or drifting down." For many readers of *A Week*, both then and now, this has been a stumbling block. The basic story was a day-by-day account of the river voyage. Thoreau eliminated the days of hiking so that the book had the greater unity of focusing on a single week on the water. The account of the boat trip is delightful and contains some of Thoreau's most beautiful and exuberant writing. But the travel narrative takes up less than half of the book. Interspersed are a wide range of essays, poems, translations, and quotations.

Some of this material, such as the discourse on the fish of New England rivers, is directly related to the voyage. Extended essays on friendship, religion, literature, and writing, on the other hand, seem to bear little relation to the narrative. Fifteen of the inserts were from material already published in the *Dial*. Most of the other inclusions were culled from his Journal, from its beginning in 1837 through 1848. In short, *A Week* is a miscellany in prose and verse, ranging from Homer to Goethe, American Indians to Greek gods.

Perhaps for these reasons, and despite the generally good reviews, the book failed to sell. In 1853, his publisher delivered to Henry 706 unsold copies out of an original printing of 1000. Thoreau quipped: "I have now a library of nearly nine hundred volumes, over seven hundred of which I wrote myself." This first venture into book publishing cost him $290.

Yet even while *A Week* did not originally reach a large audience and remains one of Thoreau's lesser-read publications, it has delighted discriminating readers for nearly a century and a half. It is the work of a young man seeking the meaning of life and the spiritual reality of nature, and it contains beautiful passages such as this:

> It required some rudeness to disturb with our boat the mirror-like surface of the water, in which every twig and blade of grass was so faithfully reflected; too faithfully indeed for art to imitate, for only Nature may exaggerate herself. The shallowest still water is unfathomable. Wherever the trees and skies are reflected there is more than Atlantic depth, and no danger of fancy running aground. We noticed that it required a separate intention of the eye, a more free and abstracted vision, to see the reflected trees and the sky, than to see the river bottom merely; and so are there manifold visions in the direction of every object, and even the most opaque reflect the heavens from their surface.

The spiritual reflection in the stream mirrored his life. He was "constantly as fresh as this river," with every moment "a new water" flooding his channel.

Like the more famous *Walden*, *A Week on the Concord and Merrimack Rivers* was Thoreau's effort to place himself in nature and to combine art and life. Some scholars have suggested that without this first book the more fully realized *Walden* would not have been possible.

True as this may be, the immediate effect of *A Week*'s commercial failure was Munroe & Co.'s refusal to bring out *Walden*.

As it turned out, the publication of *Walden* would be delayed for another five years. Yet despite Thoreau's disappointment at the time, the unwillingness of publishers to print the version of *Walden* he had written at the pond proved a blessing. Between 1849 and 1854, he made seven major manuscript revisions, each of which enriched the original without destroying its authenticity. What had begun as a fairly straightforward account of his life in the woods became a near perfect blending of art, life, and nature.

Finally, in March, 1854, nine years after Henry had begun cutting pines to build his pondside cabin, Ticknor & Fields of Boston accepted *Walden* for publication. William Ticknor and James Fields were already recognized as the outstanding publishers of American literature. Among their noted New England authors were Nathaniel Hawthorne, Henry Wadsworth Longfellow, Robert Lowell, and John Greenleaf Whittier. Now they added Thoreau.

Walden was published on August 9, 1854. The following day Thoreau's journal contained this entry: "First muskmelon in garden." But clearly he was proud of his literary accomplishment. Later that month Emerson described him as "the undoubted King of American lions. He is walking up & down Concord, firm-looking, but in a tremble of great expectation."

His pride was justified. He had written a permanent book, a tract not just for his times but for all times. *Walden* can be read on many levels. At its most basic, it is an autobiographical account of one man's experiment in living. Some see it as a kind of "how-to" manual on self-sufficiency, a personal Declaration of Independence, filled with useful advice on cabin construction, food, books, health, and nature. For others it is a romantic pastoral, extolling the virtues of country over city and filled with beautiful nature writing. Still other readers are most impressed by the book's caustic critique of capitalism and technology. *Walden* is all these things, but above all it is a story of the spiritual renewal of life. The book tells of a rebellious, despondent youth, Henry Thoreau, who leaves the society of his elders to live alone in nature. There he discovers something that prepares him to return from exile and accept his communal place. *Walden* is the symbolic account of this metamorphosis.

The book begins with Thoreau's analysis of the lives of "quiet desperation" led by his townspeople. In the long introductory chapter, "Economy," he lamented most men's dull, mechanized, materialistic existences. To Thoreau the inhabitants of Concord appeared "to be doing penance in a thousand remarkable ways." The market economy and machinery had dehumanized life. This was not simply the economic problem of "men" having "become the tools of their tools." It was even more a problem of perception. "Our vision," he maintained, "does not penetrate the surface of things." To see deeper it was necessary for the book's hero, Henry David Thoreau, to remove himself from society.

While Thoreau's critique of that society could be scathing, *Walden* was not intended to be negative. In the book's epigraph he wrote: "I do not propose to write an ode to dejection, but to brag as lustily as chanticleer [rooster] in the morning, standing on his roost, if only to wake my neighbors up." To do this it was necessary for him to withdraw from society to learn anew how to live life deeply, and, in recording that fulfilled life, to help his readers liberate themselves from the limits of their surface existences. He was a herald come to waken the world to a deeper, wiser way of life.

To tell his story with more unity and force, Thoreau compressed the two years, two months, and two days he spent at the pond into a single year. In this way, the action followed the natural cycle of the seasons, beginning with his moving in on the Fourth of July and ending with spring the following year. Thoreau's life at the pond corresponded to the seasons of nature with a symbolic pattern of growth, death, and rebirth. In summer nature was at her peak; Thoreau hoed his bean field and enjoyed the outdoor life. He learned to see and hear carefully. Autumn with its falling leaves was a time of harvesting both food and knowledge. It was also a time of drawing inward; in his first fall at the pond, he shingled his cabin, added lath and plaster to the inside walls, and built his fireplace and chimney. In winter nature lay dormant beneath ice and snow; Thoreau sat long by his fire, read, reflected and learned to be patient. But with the arrival of spring the world was born again, life was renewed. *Walden* then, was a chronicle of Thoreau's seasonal metamorphosis, his passage from a lower to a higher plane of life, his rebirth.

In addition to the symbolism of the seasons, Thoreau also employed the symbolism of the day in individual chapters. "The day," he wrote, "is an epitome of the year. The night is the winter, the morning and evening are the spring and fall, and the noon is the summer." In a lovely chapter on "Sounds," for instance, he began with the singing of birds in the afternoon, continuing through the sounds of evening and night, and ending with the cock crowing at dawn, a symbol of spring and rebirth.

While the cycles of the year and the day provided the organizing principle for *Walden*, with spring, morning, and the sun serving as symbols of spiritual awakening, the book's central symbol was Walden Pond itself. Thoreau described the pond as a "crystal well." It lay "between the earth and the heavens, it partakes of the color of both." The pond was also "a mirror which no stone can crack"; its water "full of light and reflections, becomes a lower heaven itself so much the more important."

In his chapter "The Ponds," he noted that "this pond [Walden] is remarkable for its depth and purity . . . It is a clear and deep green well, half a mile long and a mile and three quarters in circumference, and contains about sixty-one and a half acres;

Walden Pond as it appears in May, 1990. (Photo courtesy of Marcia Stern)

a perennial spring in the midst of pine and oak woods, without any visible inlet or outlet except by the clouds and evaporation."

To account for Walden's remarkable purity, depth, and lack of inlet or outlet, Thoreau concocted a fable about the pond's creation. "That ancient settler" [God], he wrote, "first came here with his divining-rod, saw a thin vapor rising from the sward [field], and the hazel pointed stead-ily downward, and he concluded to dig a well here." Walden was " 'God's Drop' ?" and a "distiller of celestial dews." Even its bottom was "pure sand." Fed by springs from deep within the earth, Walden was both "ancient" and "peren-nially young," and was for Thoreau the primary manifes-tation of the divine in nature.

Walden reflected the heavens, but also mirrored the shore and was for Thoreau an art gallery of nature's masterpieces. "Each morning the manager of this gallery substituted some new picture, distinguished by more bril-liant or harmonious coloring, for the old upon the walls." Thus the pond was "intermediary in its nature between land and sky"; it united the main elements of nature and served as a link between earth and heaven.

Walden was for Thoreau the "earth's eye; looking into which the beholder measures the depth of his own nature." The pond enabled him to perceive his own spiritual being as well as the divine in nature. In summer he often sat in his boat at the pond's center and marveled at the forest and hills "which rise from the water's edge" in perfect harmony. In winter the frozen pond presented "new views . . . of the familiar landscape."

Not all people understood Walden as Thoreau did. In the chapter "The Ponds in Winter" Thoreau recounted the myth of Walden's bottomlessness. "It is remarkable," he wrote, "how long men will believe in the bottomlessness of a pond without taking the trouble to sound it." People wished to believe in the infinite, yet never penetrated beyond the finite surface. Thoreau wanted his infinite to rest on a factual foundation. By breaking through the surface ice he soon found the bottom "with a cod-line and a stone weighing about a pound and a half." "I can assure my readers that Walden has a reasonably tight bottom at a not unreasonable, though at an unusual, depth. *I fathomed it easily.*" His spiritual truth, in other words, was grounded in reality, though he was "thankful that this pond was made deep and pure for a symbol."

Thoreau believed the true depth and purity of the pond remained incomprehensible to most people because they were not spiritually prepared to understand it. Only those individuals able to curb their base instincts could fathom the pond's true reality. Thoreau submitted himself to the pond: "Every morning was a cheerful invitation to make my life of equal simplicity, and I may say innocence, with Nature herself . . . I got up early and bathed in the pond; that was a religious exercise, and one of the best things which I did. They say that characters were engraven on the bathing tub of King Tching-thang to this effect: 'Renew thyself completely each day; do it again, and again, and forever again.'" Bathing in the pure pond water, warmed by the morning sun, Thoreau was spiritually cleansed and prepared for higher discoveries.

Yet Walden as part of nature was also subject to the cycles of the seasons. In winter, "like the marmots in the surrounding hills, it closes its eyelids and becomes dormant for three months or more." On occasion the snow-covered ice made the pond virtually indistinguishable "from any level field."

To the discerning eye, however, even in the depth of winter the pond remained a thing of wonder. Thoreau, cutting his "way first through a foot of snow, and then a foot of ice," opened "a window under my feet, where, kneeling to drink, I look down into the quiet parlor of the fishes, pervaded by a softened light as through a window of ground glass, with its bright sanded floor the same as in summer; there a perennial waveless serenity reigns as in the amber twilight sky, corresponding to the cool and even temperament of the inhabitants. Heaven is under our feet as well as over our heads."

Beneath the ice he also discovered the pickerel, a "fabulous" fish of "rare beauty." "They are not green like the pines, nor grey like the stones, nor blue like the sky; but they have, to my eyes, if possible, yet rarer colors, like flowers and precious stones, as if they were the pearls, . . .

or crystals of the Walden water. They, of course, are Walden all over and all through; are themselves small waldens in the animal kingdom, Waldenses."[1]

That same winter while probing for the pond's bottom he discovered a "bright green weed," a symbol of organic life, still undulating in the frozen pond. The green weed, responding to the sun, "stretched itself and yawned like a waking man." The stirring weed prophesied the coming spring, that inevitable time of thaw when "all things give way to the impulse of expression."

Soon the days lengthened; fogs, rains, and the ever warmer sun began to melt the pond's ice and snow. In early March the bluebirds and redwing blackbirds returned with their songs of "younger hope than ever." Woodchucks and chipmunks freed from their winter's hibernation scampered about the pondside fields and woods. Finally on March 25 the last ice melted. The water now sparkled in the sun and the pond was "full of glee and youth, as if it spoke the joy of the fishes within it, and of the sands on its shore." "Such is the contrast between winter and spring. Walden was dead," announced Thoreau, "and is alive again." Spring had come, and with it nature and humans were reborn.

Henry Thoreau was ecstatic:

> Suddenly an influx of light filled my house, though the evening was at hand, and the clouds of winter still overhung it, and the eaves were dripping with sleety rain. I looked out of the window, and lo! where yesterday was cold gray ice there lay the transparent pond already calm and full of hope as in a summer evening, reflecting a summer evening sky in its bosom, though none was visible overhead, as if it had intelligence with some remote horizon. I heard a robin in the distance, the first I had heard for many a thousand years . . . the same sweet and powerful song as of yore . . . The pitch-pines and shrub-oaks about my house, which had so long drooped, suddenly resumed their several characters, looked brighter, greener, and more erect and alive, as if effectually cleansed and re-

---

[1]Waldenses were a mystical, medieval religious sect that stressed a life of simplicity much like Thoreau.

stored by the rain . . . As it grew darker, I was startled by the *honking* of geese . . . Standing at my door, I could hear the rush of their wings . . . So I came in, and shut the door, and passed my first spring night in the woods.

Spring created the world anew. There had been no fall from God's grace. "Perhaps on that spring morning when Adam and Eve were driven out of Eden," Thoreau mused,

> Walden Pond was already in existence, and even then breaking up in a gentle spring rain accompanied with mist and a southerly wind, and covered with myriads of ducks and geese, which had not heard of the fall, when still such pure lakes sufficed them. Even then it had commenced to rise and fall, and had clarified its waters, and colored them of the hue they now wear, and obtained a patent of heaven to be the only Walden Pond in the world . . . Who knows . . . what nymphs presided over it in the Golden Age?

In "Spring," *Walden*'s climactic chapter, Thoreau witnessed the process of rebirth and the creativity of nature. This he saw reflected not only in the rejuvenation of Walden, but even in the resurrection of the inert clay bank of the Deep Cut made by the railroad along one edge of the pond. The freezing and thawing of early spring caused a "bursting out" of the "insides of the earth" in elaborate patterns of "luxuriant foliage." Thoreau watched this process in awe, feeling himself to be a witness to creation itself:

> I am affected as if in a peculiar sense I stood in the laboratory of the Artist who made the world and me,—had come to where he was still at work, sporting on this bank, and with excess of energy strewing his fresh designs about. I feel as if I were nearer to the vitals of the globe, for this sandy overflow is something such a foliaceous [leaflike] mass as the vitals of the animal body. You find thus in the very sands an anticipation of the vegetable leaf. No wonder that the earth expresses itself outwardly in leaves, it so labors with the idea inwardly.

Observing this pageant of life arising out of inorganic matter, Thoreau concluded: "There is nothing inorganic."

Having experienced the joys of spiritual renewal in the spring of nature, he returned to society and challenged his neighbors to live their lives to the fullest. Life in the woods beside the pure pond had taught him to live with integrity and higher purpose. He learned to cherish freedom, to respect the laws of nature and to see beneath and above the surface of things to an essential Reality.

Walden closed with the fable of "a strong and beautiful bug which came out of the dry leaf of an old table of apple-tree wood, which had stood in a farmer's kitchen for sixty years." In writing of this miracle Thoreau reiterated the theme of organic renewal: "Who knows what beautiful and winged life, whose egg has been buried for ages under many concentric layers of woodenness in the dead dry life of society, deposited at first in the alburnum of the green and living tree, which has been gradually converted into the semblance of its well-seasoned tomb . . . may unexpectedly come forth from amidst society's most trivial and handselled furniture, to enjoy its perfect summer life at last!"

It was not too late for people in society to become liberated from their shallow, materialistic lives. *Walden*'s last lines returned to the symbols of spiritual awakening—water, morning, and sun: "The life in us is like the water in the river. It may rise this year higher than man has ever known it, and flood the parched uplands; even this may be the eventful year . . . It was not always dry land where we dwell . . . Such is the character of that morrow which mere lapse of time can never make to dawn. The light which puts out our eyes is darkness to us. Only that day dawns to which we are awake. There is more day to dawn. The sun is but a morning star."

7

THE TRAVELER

We have advanced by leaps to the Pacific,
and left many a lesser Oregon and
California unexplored behind us.
                              —*The Maine Woods*

America has long been a nation of travelers, and perhaps at no time was this more true than in the 1840s and 1850s. Lured by hopes of wealth and adventure, thousands of people pushed westward. They settled the great prairies of the Middle West; they wrested Texas and the Southwest from Mexico; they crossed the continent by covered wagon to farm and fish in the Oregon Territory. In 1846 and 1847, thousands of Mormons marched across the desert seeking the promised land in the basin of Utah's Great Salt Lake. A year later in 1848 the discovery of gold near Sacramento brought the rush of fortune-hunting forty-niners to California.

Young writers and artists, too, had the itch to roam. Thoreau's Harvard classmate, Richard Henry Dana, sailed around the world and produced a classic account of his adventure in *Two Years Before the Mast* (1840). While the 24-year-old Thoreau was moving in with Emerson in 1841, the 22-year-old Herman Melville was voyaging to the South Seas and would later recount his exploits in *Typee* (1846), *Omoo* (1847) and *Mardi* (1849). In 1846, while Thoreau lived on the outskirts of Concord at Walden Pond, Francis Parkman, a recent Harvard graduate, was off studying nature and the Indian tribes of the Far West; he would go on to publish his findings in *The Oregon Trail* (1849).

Henry Thoreau, soon after resigning his Concord teaching job in 1837, had thought of going West to look for a position in

Kentucky. This never came to pass, and except for his brief residence on Staten Island in 1843, he lived his life in Concord, mostly in his parents' house. Thoreau was ambivalent about travel. He obviously loved Concord and saw its natural environs as a microcosm in which he could "explore and learn all things." "It takes a man of genius," he commented, "to travel in his own country, in his native village; to make any progress between his door and his gate." In this respect, he was one of the more parochial of America's great 19th-century literary figures.

Yet he was fascinated about faraway places and loved reading accounts of travelers in exotic lands. Melville's *Typee* greatly impressed him. He was also concerned that Concord was becoming too civilized. He grieved the disappearance of wild animals such as the cougar, wolf, and moose, and lamented in his Journal that "I cannot but feel as if I lived in a tamed, and, as it were emasculated country."

Family responsibilities, lack of money, and his fondness for Concord prevented him from venturing too far afield for very long. But genuine wilderness could be found close at hand. Thoreau's "lesser Oregon and California" were the wilds of Maine and Canada, and there was wilderness of a different sort along the wind-swept, sea-battered beaches of Cape Cod. Thoreau made three trips to Maine, four to Cape Cod and one to Canada. These travels in turn became the subjects of lectures, magazine essays and ultimately three posthumously published books: *The Maine Woods* (1864), *Cape Cod* (1865) and *A Yankee in Canada* (1866).

He took his first Maine excursion, other than the brief job-hunting trip he made in 1838, in the summer of 1846 while he resided at Walden. Having recently read of a geological expedition to Mount Katahdin, Maine's highest peak, Thoreau was eager to climb it. He also wished to confront a wilder world than he had yet experienced and to know first hand the ways of the Indian.

Leaving Boston by steamer on August 31, he arrived in Bangor the next day where he was met by his cousin, George Thatcher, an outdoorsman who was in the lumber business. Departing Bangor by horse-drawn buggy, they stopped first in Old Town where Thatcher made arrangements to hire Indian guides while the fascinated Thoreau watched Indians making canoes.

When the two reached the designated meeting site no Indians were to be found. Thoreau learned later that their would-be guides had gone off on a drinking spree. Still determined to press on they hired two backwoods whites, George McCauslin and Tom Fowler. Soon they were being poled in a double-ended, flat-bottomed bateau up the West Branch of the Penobscot River and later the Millinocket River, traveling with a speed that reminded Thoreau of salmon swimming up rapids. After several days of poling, rowing, portaging, and camping, they arrived at Sowadnehunk Deadwater, about 12 miles from the summit of Katahdin. Setting out the next morning they hiked across wild country toward the mountain. By 4:00 P.M. they were in view of the summit and decided to camp, though the ever eager Thoreau continued climbing for a time in a futile effort to reach the top before dark. The next morning the party renewed the difficult climb. Thoreau alone was successful, having left his less energetic companions behind. He ascended the exacting route directly up the south peak. At the time he was one of only a few whites who had ever climbed the 5,268 foot Katahdin. Having accomplished this, he soon rejoined the others and within two days was back in Bangor where he caught the Boston steamer on September 11.

Seven years later, in September, 1853, Thoreau returned to Maine. This time Thatcher had succeeded in engaging an Indian guide, Joe Aitteon, the son of the Penobscot governor. Traveling by coach to Greenville at the southern end of Moosehead Lake, they then took a small steamer the length of the lake where they set out by canoe north on the West Branch of the Penobscot to Chesuncook Lake. On this trip Thatcher shot a moose, the first Thoreau had ever seen.

Retracing their route they camped one night with a group of Indians who were busy curing moose hides and smoking the meat. Thoreau asked them innumerable questions and was most pleased to spend the night in an Indian camp. Two days later they were back in Bangor, but before sailing for Boston, Thoreau spent a day in Old Town interviewing Indians and again watching them build canoes.

His final Maine adventure took place during the last week of July and the first week of August, 1857. This time he was

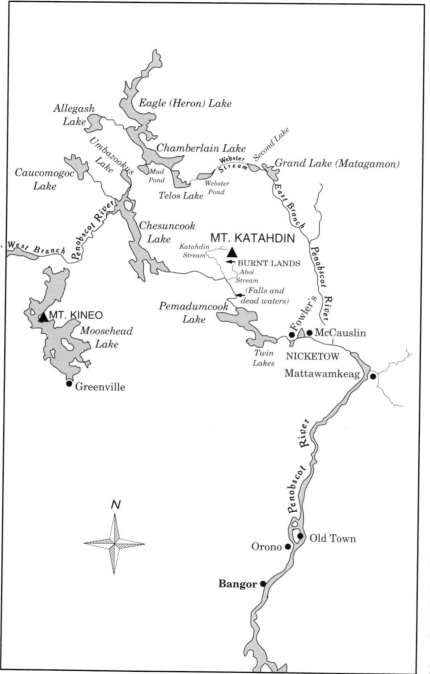

Allegash Lake

Eagle (Heron) Lake

Umbazookus Lake

Chamberlain Lake

Second Lake

Webster Stream

Grand Lake (Matagamon)

Caucomogoc Lake

Mud Pond

Webster Pond

Telos Lake

East Branch

Penobscot River

Chesuncook Lake

West Branch

MT. KATAHDIN

Katahdin Stream

BURNT LANDS

Abol Stream

(Falls and dead waters)

Pemadumcook Lake

Penobscot River

MT. KINEO

Fowler's

McCauslin

Moosehead Lake

Twin Lakes

NICKETOW

Mattawamkeag

Greenville

N

Penobscot River

Orono

Old Town

Bangor

Map of the Maine Woods trip. (William Howarth, The Book of Concord, p. 142) accompanied by Edward Hoar, whose last outing with Thoreau had resulted in the burning of Concord woods. Hoar, now a lawyer, had recently returned from the wilds of California and was eager to test his woodcraft in Maine. Again an Indian guide was hired, a 48-year-old Penobscot named Joe Polis. This trip took them to some of the same places Thoreau had visited in 1853. They journeyed to Greenville and went the length of Moosehead, though this time in Polis' heavily loaded canoe. Once more they made their way to Chesuncook. Then they went further, canoeing and portaging to Chamberlain Lake and the lakes that form the headwaters of the Allegash River. Finally turning back they traveled to the East Branch of the Penobscot via Webster Brook where the water was so treacherous that Thoreau and Hoar had to struggle with heavy packs through dense forests while Polis ran the rapids in his canoe. Eleven days after they had left they arrived back at the Penobscot Indian reservation in Old Town, 12 miles north of Bangor. All told they had canoed some 325 miles.

This had been Thoreau's longest and in many ways harshest wilderness experience. But it was also his most satisfying ordeal in the wild, due especially to his association with Polis, whom he described as belonging to the "aristocracy" of his tribe. Polis would remain one of Henry's heroes. Thoreau had also proved himself most capable in the wild. Hoar would later write of his "courage and manliness": "nobody who had seen him among the Penobscot rocks and rapids, the Indian trusting his life and his canoe to his skill, promptitude, and nerve, would ever doubt it."

As was his usual practice, Thoreau took notes on each of these trips. Back in Concord he turned this material into lectures and eventually essays. "Ktaadn," Thoreau's spelling of Katahdin and the account of his first trip, was delivered as a lecture at the Concord Lyceum in January, 1848. Later that year it was published as a five-part serial in *Sartain's Union Magazine*.

"Chesuncook," the narrative of his second journey, was given as a lecture in December, 1853, and published by James Russell Lowell in the *Atlantic Monthly* in three installments in 1858. He was still revising the essay on his last trip, "The Allegash and East Branch," at the time of his death in 1862. Ellery Channing and Thoreau's sister, Sophia, collected all three essays and had Ticknor and Fields issue them as a book, *The Maine Woods*, in 1864.

Less complex than either *A Week* or *Walden*, *The Maine Woods* is a very pleasant narrative. Anyone who has canoed or backpacked in the wilds will be stirred by Thoreau's superb descriptions, his vivid recreations of the atmosphere of forest and stream, and his unobtrusive inclusions of natural science and history. Though the three essays that make up the book recount separate trips, there is a thematic unity to *The Maine Woods*.

The book's two major themes are the wilderness and the Indian. Naively, Thoreau had assumed before his first trip to Katahdin that in Maine he would encounter primitive forests inhabited by primitive men. "If wild men . . . have inhabited these shores before us," he wrote, should not one know "particularly what nature of men they are, how they lived there [and] their relations to nature?" He hoped to experience the New World as the first European settlers had found it.

He was quickly disillusioned. Instead of some noble savage, the first Indian he encountered was a "short, shabby washerwoman-looking Indian" holding an empty liquor keg. Looking about the Penobscot reservation he was saddened to see how many Indians had adopted white people's ways; he described their houses as having a "forlorn, cheerless look" like those of many of his neighbors back in Massachusetts. His disenchantment was further intensified when the Indian guides he and Thatcher had hired to go to Katahdin failed to keep their promised rendezvous.

His initial view of the Maine forest was also a dissatisfying one. Intensive lumbering had denuded much of the original wilderness. "Ktaadn" begins with a condemnation of the lumbering industry. "Think how stood the white pine tree on the shore of Chesuncook, its boughs soughing with the four winds, and every individual needle trembling in the sunlight—think how it stands with it now—sold, perchance, to the New England Friction-Match Company!" He satirized lumbermen as "10,000 vermin gnawing at the base of her [the wilderness'] noblest trees." "The mission of men," he went on, "seems to be, like so many busy demons, to drive the forest all out of the country, from every solitary beaver swamp, and mountain side."

Yet he did ultimately encounter both real wilderness and untainted natives. His reaction to each would be ambivalent, though ultimately positive. On his first trip when his party entered North Twin Lake he realized they had passed beyond civilization. There were no roads and no houses. They were "completely surrounded by the forest as savage and impassable now as to the first adventurers." Here nature was not like the benevolent, pastoral shores of Walden Pond.

In his descriptions of wilderness throughout *The Maine Woods* there lurks an element of fear. The forests were "grim" and "dark." They closed in about one so that it was impossible to see more than a few feet ahead. Coming upon a small cleared farm surrounded by dense forest, Thoreau imagined that the inhabitants walked about "in their clearing somewhat as in a prison-yard."

He and his companions suffered many personal hardships on these trips. At one point, Thoreau described a portage he and Hoar made with 60-pound packs after having lost their way and their Indian guide:

> We then entered another swamp, at a necessarily slow pace, where the walking was worse than ever, not only on account of the water, but the fallen timber, which often obliterate the indistinct trail entirely. The fallen trees were so numerous, that for long distances the route was through a succession of small yards, where we climbed over fences as high as our heads, down into water often up to our knees, and then over another fence into a second yard, and so on; going back for his bag my companion once lost his way and came back without it.

They encountered swarms of mosquitoes, black flies, no-see-ems, and moose flies. Thoreau even preferred nights when it rained hard because that kept the bugs down. While nature at Walden gave him a sense of freedom, often in Maine it made him shudder. So wild was some of the country, he noted, that "at a hundred rods [from camp] you might be lost past recovery." Indeed Hoar did get lost and spent a frightful, foodless night alone while Henry fretted about what he "could do in such a wilderness," and how Hoar's "relatives would feel, if I should return without him."

Thoreau came to recognize in Maine how utterly indifferent to human life nature was. This had been impressed upon him on his first trip when he climbed Katahdin alone. He described the mountaintop as "vast, Titanic, and such as man never inhabits," and came to the realization that he was in the presence of "ancient Demonic Nature . . . nature primitive— powerful gigantic aweful and beautiful, Untamed forever."

Yet even the harshest trials on such outings, though frightening, were also exhilarating. The terrors of the densest forest or the bleakest mountain peak often inspired Thoreau with a sense of awe. There was a power and grandeur in such scenes that deepened his veneration of "nature primitive."

It was also in such wild "recesses" that Thoreau hoped to come to know the Indian. His fascination with native Americans went back to his childhood when he and his brother used to pretend to be Indians. They also searched for, and frequently found, arrowheads and other artifacts of the original inhabitants of New England. While Hawthorne and other writers lamented the absence of antiquities in America, Thoreau found evidence of ancient life all about. He came to identify the Indian as the central figure in the drama of American history.

Thoreau lived in the age of ruthless Indian Removal. Beginning with the presidency of Andrew Jackson from 1829 to 1837, and continuing through subsequent administrations, it became official federal policy to force the major eastern Indian tribes to the West. Many died en route. Those who resisted were annihilated. Placed on supposedly permanent reservations, the Indians were frequently forced to move whenever whites discovered valuable resources on tribal land. To most 19th-century Americans the Indian was a "savage" who would have to give way before the advance of white civilization even if this meant the extermination of the race. In a very popular novel, *Nick of the Woods*, published in 1837, the year of Henry's graduation from Harvard, author Robert Bird depicted the killing of Indians as heroic adventure. In addition to becoming a pattern for a whole genre of violent westerns, Bird's novel also coined what became a favored phrase: "The only good Indian is a dead Indian."

Henry Thoreau was one of a minority of Americans free from such bloodthirsty racism. He viewed native Americans as the noble and legitimate inhabitants of the continent and believed they had a great deal to teach the white race. He was especially fascinated by the Indians' closeness to nature. "They seem like a race who have exhausted the secrets of nature, tanned with age . . . their memory is in harmony with the russet hue of the fall of the year." Given Thoreau's critical assessment of the civilization of white America, it is not surprising that he opposed "civilizing" native Americans.

> We talk of civilizing the Indian, but that is not the name for his improvement. By the wary independence and aloofness of his dim forest life he preserves his intercourse with his native gods, and is admitted from time to time to a rare and peculiar society with Nature . . . If we could listen but for an instant to the chant of the Indian muse, we should understand why he will not exchange his savageness for civilization . . . Steel and blankets are strong temptations; but the Indian does well to continue Indian.

While Thoreau's views were not without bias, he approached the study of the Indian with humility and decency. After his initial disappointing encounters with some Penobscots on his first trip to Maine, he increasingly immersed himself in the study of Indian life. He was especially interested in the first contact between whites and natives, the meeting point between wilderness life and European civilization. He systematically read various accounts by early explorers and settlers as well as more recent studies on the subject. He planned to write a major book on American Indians. Unfortunately, he died before this came to pass, leaving behind 11 unpublished notebooks totalling more than 2,800 pages.

His scholarly research gave Thoreau a greater understanding of Indian life than most people possessed. But even more important to him was his actual contact with Indians during his last two Maine trips. Thoreau became close to Joe Aitteon, the guide on his second visit. But it was Joe Polis who most impressed him.

The final section of *The Maine Woods*, "The Allegash and East Branch," fully and subtly develops Polis' character. Though a sophisticated Indian who had represented his tribe in Washington, D.C. and had met Daniel Webster, Polis had not been spoiled by civilization. He was skilled at woodcraft and totally at home in the wild. He could shoot rapids, talk to muskrats, and find his way anywhere in the forest without compass or map. "He does not carry things in his head, nor remember the route exactly, like a white man," wrote Thoreau, "but relies on himself at the moment." The characterization of Polis is as authentic and appealing as any portrayal of a native American by a white writer in 19th-century America. This alone makes *The Maine Woods* well worth reading today.

Thoreau's last two travel books, *Cape Cod* and *A Yankee in Canada*, though less significant than *Maine*, are nonetheless

Thoreau the traveler as he would have appeared to Cape Coders, from a pencil sketch by Daniel Ricketson. (Author's collection)

interesting reading. Between 1849 and 1857, Thoreau made four trips to Cape Cod, twice with Ellery Channing and twice alone. Unlike the separate accounts of his Maine expeditions, he used his first excursion on the Cape as the framework for his book, inserting incidents from later visits as best he could. The result is an integrated travel narrative that remains one of the best books written about the Cape.

Cape Cod in Thoreau's day was different from the tourist-ridden ocean playground of recent times. Then there were no summer homes and only a few small hotels and boarding houses where a traveler might spend a night. This was the historic Cape where weatherbeaten men and care-worn women, descendants of the original Pilgrims, eked out a living from the sea. They were provincial, suspicious people. On one occasion Thoreau, walking with his umbrella and bag, was mistaken for a bank robber; another time he was thought to be a troublesome peddler.

Thoreau was adept at capturing the people and customs of the place. In *Cape Cod* one gets glimpses of women hanging flounders on their clotheslines to dry; of split, salted cod "stacked up on the wharves, looking like corded wood, maple and yellow birch with the bark left on"; of mackerel fleets setting sail before a light breeze in the early morning. There are charming and humorous vignettes of retired sea captains, widows, village eccentrics. Two of the longest and best of these character sketches portray a quirky, old Wellfleet oysterman and the keeper of the Highland lighthouse.

Thoreau interspersed his contemporary narrative with fascinating historical material. He had read various accounts about the Cape ranging from Pilgrim chronicles to 19th-century guidebooks. He also included detailed and accurate descriptions of the area's flora and fauna with its cranberry bogs, swamps, beach grasses, and dwarf forests.

Here Thoreau's writing style, except for an occasional quotation in Greek, is direct, descriptive, and often humorous. Character studies, uncommon scenes, natural science, and local history flow together in a light, entertaining manner. These qualities have led critics to call *Cape Cod* "Thoreau's sunniest book" and "the most human of his books." It is not surprising, therefore, that it is still commonly stocked in tourist shops from Plymouth to Provincetown.

Yet for all its light-heartedness, *Cape Cod* is also a serious and somber book. The account begins, as did his first trip, with a disturbing disaster: "On reaching Boston, we found that the Provincetown steamer, which should have got in the day before, had not yet arrived, on account of a violent storm; and, as we noticed in the streets a handbill headed, 'Death! one hundred and forty five lives lost at Cohasset,' we decided to go by way of Cohasset." Thoreau and Channing arrived two days after the brig *St. John*, packed with Irish immigrants, had broken up on rocks in a fierce gale. The waves were still high and bodies were still being swept ashore. Thoreau saw

> many marble feet and matted heads as the clothes were raised, and one livid, swollen, and mangled body of a drowned girl,—who probably had intended to go out to service in some American family,—to which some rags still adhered, with a string, half concealed by the flesh, about its swollen neck; the coiled up wreck of a human hulk, gashed by the rocks or fishes, so that the bone and muscle were exposed, but quite bloodless,—merely red and white, with wide open and staring eyes, yet lustreless, dead lights.

This opening scene of mass death caused by a ferocious and indifferent ocean is a theme that runs through the book. Here was a different wilderness, the "unwearied and illimitable ocean." Thoreau's Cape is a place where life is at the mercy of the sea. "It is a wild, rank place, and there is no flattery in it." The beach is

> strewn with crabs, horseshoes, and razor clams, and whatever the sea casts up,—a vast *morgue*, where famished dogs may range in packs, and crows come daily to glean the pittance which the tide leaves them. The carcasses of men and beasts together lie stately up upon its shelf, rotting and bleaching in the sun and waves, and each tide turns them in their beds, and tucks fresh sand under them. There is naked Nature,—inhumanly sincere, wasting no thought on man, nibbling at the cliffy shore where gulls wheel amid the spray.

Even the land itself is but wave-washed, wind-blown sand held tenuously by "myriad little cables of beach grass."

Thoreau had gone to Cape Cod, as he said in the first sentence of the book, "to get a better view than I had yet had of the ocean, which, we are told, covers more than two thirds of the globe, but of which a man who lives a few miles inland may never see any trace, more than of another world." He was the outsider who found a seashore "where man's works are wrecks" and "where the crumbling land is the only invalid."

Even more than atop Mount Katahdin, Thoreau felt humbled by the awesome power and mysteriousness of the sea. "We do not associate the idea of antiquity with the ocean," he wrote,

> nor wonder how it looked a thousand years ago, as we do of the land, for it was equally wild and unfathomable always. The Indians have left no traces on its surface, but it is the same to the civilized man and the savage. The aspect of the shore only has changed. The ocean is a wilderness reaching round the globe, wilder than a Bengal jungle, and fuller of monsters, washing the very wharves of our cities and the gardens of our sea-side residences. Serpents, bears, hyenas, tigers, rapidly vanish as civilization advances, but the most populous and civilized city cannot scare a shark far from its wharves.

Thoreau concluded that he "was a land animal," but certainly his ocean experiences tempered his transcendental optimism and left him with a more complex view of nature.

The last of Thoreau's excursion books, *A Yankee in Canada*, is his least successful. The opening lines read: "I fear that I have not got much to say about Canada, not having seen much; what I got by going to Canada was a cold." In late September, 1850, he and Channing joined some 1,500 other Yankes on a 10-day tour of Canada that a railroad offered at the special rate of $7. They went by train to Burlington, Vermont, crossed Lake Champlain by steamer, took another train from Plattsburg, New York to Montreal, and then by steamer went on to Quebec with side trips to St. Anne de Beaupre and Montmorency Falls.

Thoreau had a genuine and longstanding interest in Canada. He was fascinated by the early French explorers and fur traders and their relations with the Indians. He read early chronicles, travelers accounts, guidebooks and histories, including the voluminous reports the 17th-century Jesuits had made concerning their mission to the Indians.

But the Canada of his scholarly focus was not the Canada he encountered on his brief tour. His preoccupation was with the wilderness world of noble Indians and heroic white adventurers. What he found was "a rather poor-looking race, clad in gray homespun, which gave them the appearance of being covered with dust." At home in the country, this trip focused on cities. Thoreau was not pleased. Though highly critical of society in America, this first visit to a foreign country brought out the latent nationalist in him. Everything about Canada seemed different and inferior to what he knew in New England. He found that the people were lazy and lacked the spirit of Yankee enterprise. Their institutions, too, seemed backward, less developed than those he found in Massachusetts.

Above all he was appalled by the commanding presence of the Catholic Church and the English military. Everywhere he went there were priests, nuns and soldiers. Every city and village in French Canada appeared to be dominated by huge stone cathedrals and fortifications. In Montreal he visited Notre Dame, the largest church in North America. Though impressed by its cave-like feeling and "the quiet religious atmosphere of the place," he assured his readers that "in Concord . . . we do not need such. Our forests are such a church, far grander and more sacred." He condemned Catholic education as a process "not of enlightening, but of obfuscating the mind." Though anti-Catholic bias was commonplace in Thoreau's New England, he was really more anticlerical than anti-Catholic. "I am sure but this Catholic religion would be an admirable one," he wrote, "if the priests were quite omitted."

But if there was a certain ambivalence about his attitude toward the Church, the pacifistic Thoreau was unequivocal in his condemnation of the British military stationed throughout French Canada. He referred to the well-drilled soldiers as "peculiarly destitute of originality and independence," and added, "it is impossible to give the soldier a good education, without making him a deserter." Upon witnessing the gigantic stone fortifications of Quebec City he noted that the regiment's motto was "In time of peace prepare for war," but peace he complained, "was plainly an uninvited guest."

A Yankee in Canada remains Thoreau's least read book, and unsurprisingly so. In it he dwelled so much on walls and soldiers that the reader feels caged and subjugated. It was only in the last part, with his lyrical description of the great St. Lawrence River and its early explorers who used it as a gateway to the New World, that the reader regains a sense of freedom and beauty.

8

THE REFORMER

Much has been said about American slavery, but I think that we do not even yet realize what slavery is. If I were seriously to propose to Congress to make mankind into sausages, I have no doubt that most of the members would smile at my proposition, and if any believed me to be in earnest, they would think that I proposed something much worse than Congress had ever done. But if any of them will tell me that to make a man into a sausage would be much worse,—would be any worse,—than to make him into a slave,—than it was to enact the Fugitive Slave Law,—I will accuse him of foolishness, of intellectual incapacity, of making a distinction without a difference. The one is just as sensible a proposition as the other.

—"Slavery in Massachusetts"

During the years of Thoreau's adult life, from the 1830s to the Civil War, America witnessed the most ardent and diverse outburst of reform activity in its history. All sorts of moral wrongs and social injustices came under scrutiny. People united in a wide variety of voluntary organizations to advocate temperance, world peace, health reform, women's rights, better working conditions, free public education, and, above all, the abolition of slavery.

Nowhere was reform more in evidence than in Massachusetts with Boston at the hub and nearby Concord in the forefront as well. Henry Thoreau's family shared this commitment.

His mother, Cynthia, and his Aunt Maria were charter members of the Concord chapter of the Women's Anti-Slavery Society. Also active in this cause were Henry's sisters, Helen and Sophia, and his friend, Prudence Ward, who lived in the household. The family subscribed to William Lloyd Garrison's *Liberator*, and among the boarders the Thoreaus took in were a number of reformers.

Henry did not entirely share this enthusiasm for reform. In his journal he complained of how reformers "rubbed you continually with the greasy cheeks of their kindness. They would not keep their distance, but cuddle up and lie spoon-fashion with you, no matter how hot the weather nor how narrow the bed." When Thoreau disagreed with a particularly pesky advocate he was told: "Henry, I know all you would say; I understand you perfectly; you need not explain anything to me." When another reformer added: "I am going to dive into Henry's inmost depths," Thoreau quipped, "I trust you will not strike your head against the bottom." In *Walden* he described such "self-styled reformers" as "the greatest bores" he knew.

His quarrel with reformers was not simply the result of his encounters with unpleasant supporters of various causes. As a transcendentalist, Thoreau believed that real reform could only come from within oneself. "The true reform," he wrote "can be undertaken any morning before unbarring our doors. It calls no convention . . . When an individual takes a sincere step, then all the gods attend, and his single deed is sweet." As he saw it, many of the noble causes of the age were being led by individuals who had never experienced real self-awareness. Of one such person he wrote, "here's a man who can't butter his own bread, and he has just combined with a thousand like him to make a dipt toast for all eternity." For these reasons, Thoreau had an innate distrust of any organization, however just its goals. "Nothing," he claimed, "can be effected but by one man. He who wants help wants everything."

Though Thoreau remained true to his word and never joined any reform group, he was nevertheless a reformer whose life was an embodiment of many of the leading causes of the age. Health reformers were advocating a vegetarian diet, cold water baths and outdoor exercise; Thoreau basically followed such a regimen. The temperance movement called for abstaining from alcohol, tobacco, and other stimulants; Thoreau neither drank nor smoked and seldom took anything more stimulating than an occasional cup of tea or hot chocolate. He was a pacifist and agreed with the basic principles of the peace movement. His views on the capitalist system put him in the forefront of economic and labor reform. His educational experiments and ideas were not only reformist but well in advance of his age.

While most aspects of Thoreau's life and thought reflected a progressive perspective, the cause which most concerned him was the abolishment of slavery. The abolitionist movement, launched by Garrison and others in the early 1830s, was by the 1840s the most significant reform in America. Thousands of dedicated men and women, whites and blacks, united in condemnation of the southern slave system. Motivated by Christian ethics and the ideals of American democracy, they spoke out strongly against slavery in an effort to convert Americans to the justice of their cause.

Abolitionism was a radical movement and was not only hated by southern slaveholders, but by millions of Northerners as well. Racial prejudice was nearly universal in the America of the 1830s and 1840s. Even in Boston where antislavery sentiment was widespread, Garrison was nearly killed by an angry lynch mob who dragged him through the streets with a rope about his neck. Despite frequent anti-abolitionist violence, the movement grew and continued its efforts to persuade the nation that slavery was a moral wrong and a violation of America's professed democratic creed.

Though he never joined an abolitionist organization, Thoreau needed no moral persuasion to recognize the evil of human bondage. Raised in an abolitionist household, naturally sympathetic toward all downtrodden people, he hated slavery and fought against it throughout his life in his own way.

On August 1, 1844, the antislavery women of Concord had persuaded Emerson to deliver an address commemorating the 10th anniversary of the emancipation of the slaves in the British West Indies. But when it came time to gather people for the speech, the sexton of the First Parish church refused to ring the town bell, nor would the town selectmen. Hearing of this, Thoreau rushed in, grabbed the rope, and rang the bell vigorously until a large crowd had gathered to hear Emerson's first abolitionist speech. Soon after, Thoreau arranged to have Emerson's remarks published as a pamphlet.

Less than a year later, in March, 1845, Concord was again divided over the slavery issue. On March 1, outgoing United States President John Tyler signed a bill annexing Texas. Among northern abolitionists this was correctly assessed as both a prelude to war with Mexico and a major victory for the slave states. Amidst heated local debate over slavery and the Texas question, Thoreau invited the noted abolitionist Wendell Phillips to address the Concord Lyceum. Twice before at Thoreau's request Phillips had spoken in Concord. This time the famed orator met with controversy. Three conservative curators on the Lyceum board tried to block his appearance. They were voted down and resigned in a huff, only to be replaced by Thoreau, Emerson and another antislavery advocate, Samuel Barrett.

With freedom of speech won, Phillips delivered a magnificent address on March 11, condemning slavery and the annexation of Texas. So moved was Thoreau by Phillips's words that he wrote a long letter to the *Liberator* the next day in praise of Phillips. This was soon published in Garrison's paper.

One of those to whom Phillips had referred in his lecture was Frederick Douglass, an escaped slave who had become one of the most eloquent abolitionist speakers. Thoreau had heard Douglass and greatly admired him. Phillips revealed that Douglass was in the process of writing his autobiography. He would tell the world his real name and the actual circumstances of his life as a slave, even though to do so was risking recapture. In late May, the *Narrative of the Life of Frederick Douglass an American Slave* was published. It was Douglass's declaration of freedom and one of the most moving slave narratives ever written. Soon after the *Narrative* appeared, Thoreau asserted his own freedom by moving to Walden Pond.

Yet Walden was no escape from the issues of the day. Even there the slavery controversy intruded. On one occasion Bronson Alcott and his family visited Henry at his cabin accompanied by a fugitive slave whom Thoreau assisted in making his escape. This was not the first time he had served in this capacity. Thoreau was a "conductor" on the Underground Railroad, and on numerous occasions he concealed escaped slaves in the family home and assisted them to freedom in Canada, often buying their tickets himself and escorting them on part of the journey.

Alcott, who also hated slavery, had been protesting by not paying his poll tax, a Massachusetts levy assessed on all adult males. Well before his move to Walden, Thoreau too had ceased paying this tax. Both men were dissenting from a state they believed to be in connivance with the slave system. They were incensed when the United States declared war on Mexico in May, 1846, and particularly horrified when Massachusetts dutifully complied in supplying troops for this war which Thoreau and other abolitionists saw as an unjustified conflict aimed at extending slavery into the Southwest.

In July, 1846, an incident occurred which deepened Thoreau's thinking about his relationship to a state whose actions he disapproved. One evening he walked from his pond into Concord to pick up a shoe that he had left at the cobbler's shop. On entering the town, he was approached by Sam Staples, the local constable, jailer, and tax collector. When Staples asked him to pay his tax, Thoreau answered that he had not paid it as a matter of principle and did not intend to pay it now. "Henry, if you don't pay," said Staples, "I shall have to lock you up pretty soon." "As well now as any time, Sam," came the answer. "Well, come along then," replied Staples, and he led Thoreau off to the local jail.

Henry was in jail only one night. Someone, probably his Aunt Maria, paid his tax, and in the morning Mr. Staples released the prisoner. Thoreau left, picked up his mended shoe, and within a short time he was back picking huckleberries on a hill where, he rejoiced, "the State was nowhere to be seen."

The incident inspired Thoreau to write "Civil Disobedience"—a powerful statement justifying resistance to unprincipled authority. In this essay, Thoreau asked: "How does it become a man to behave toward this American government to-day?" He answered "that he cannot without disgrace be associated with it. I cannot for an instant recognize that political organization as *my* government which is the *slave's* government also . . . This people must cease to hold slaves, and to make war on Mexico, though it cost them their existence as a people."

The problem posed by Thoreau was an age-old one—what was a person of conscience to do when confronted by institutionalized injustice? His answer was both moral and radical. He pleaded for nonviolent resistance:

> Under a government which imprisons any unjustly, the true place for a just man is also a prison . . . A minority is powerless while it conforms to the majority; it is not even a minority then; but it is irresistible when it clogs by its whole weight. If the alternative is to keep all just men in prison, or give up war and slavery, the State will not hesitate which to choose. If a thousand men were not to pay their tax-bills this year, that would not be a violent and bloody measure, as it would be to pay them, and enable the State to commit violence and shed innocent blood. This is, in fact, the definition of a peaceable revolution, if any such is possible.

Thoreau would not be satisfied "until the State comes to recognize the individual as a higher and independent power, from which all its own power and authority are derived, and treats him accordingly." As Thoreau saw it the sovereignty of individual judgment was the very basis of democracy, the rule of, by and for the people. This appeal to individual conscience has led some scholars to attack Thoreau as an anarchist. Such critics point to Thoreau's statement "that government is best which governs not at all." But Thoreau meant this as an ideal that would only be possible if all people were truly enlightened. He realized this was not the case and that government would remain for the foreseeable future a necessary expedient: "practically and as a citizen [I ask] not at once no government, but *at once* a better government."

Published originally in 1849, "Civil Disobedience" at first attracted little attention. Since that time, however, it has influenced the course of world history. Mohandas Gandhi, having read "Civil Disobedience" and *Walden* as a young man, based his successful campaign for Indian independence on the concept of civil resistance. The British Labour party in the early 20th century published "Civil Disobedience" as a guide to political action. During World War II Thoreau's essay inspired resistance movements throughout Nazi occupied Europe.

In more recent times, millions of people worldwide find themselves indebted to Thoreau's philosophy of nonviolent resistance to evil. The American civil rights and peace movements of the 1950s and 1960s drew particular inspiration from Thoreau. The late Reverend Martin Luther King, Jr. left this tribute:

> During my early college days I read Thoreau's essay on civil disobedience for the first time. Fascinated by the idea of refusing to cooperate with an evil system, I was so deeply moved that I re-read the work several times. I became convinced then that non-cooperation with evil is as much a moral obligation as is cooperation with good. No other person has been more eloquent and passionate in getting this idea across than Henry David Thoreau. As a result of his writings and personal witness we are the heirs of a legacy of creative protest. It goes without saying that the teachings of Thoreau are alive today, indeed, they are more alive today than ever before. Whether expressed in a sit-in at lunch counters, a freedom ride into Mississippi, a peaceful protest in Albany, Georgia, a bus boycott in Montgomery, Alabama, it is the outgrowth of Thoreau's insistence that evil must be resisted and no moral man can patiently adjust to injustice.

The Mexican War and Thoreau's night in jail convinced him that detachment from the greater issues of the age was impossible. "Civil Disobedience" was an eloquent effort to awaken society to the injustice of the war and the immorality of slavery, and to provide that society with a peaceful means of confronting the state. At the time few heard and even fewer heeded his message. The power of the slaveholding states over national government only seemed to increase in the late 1840s and 1850s. Sectional conflict also intensified, and by mid-century threatened the very existence of the Union. Alarmed at this, moderates in Congress pushed through a series of bills aimed at appeasing both North and South. Yet this Compromise of 1850, as it was called, satisfied neither section, and particularly alarmed the North.

The most important concession to the South was the Fugitive Slave Law that gave the federal government authority to seize fugitive slaves and to send them back to the South. Civilian onlookers were required to help federal authorities arrest fugitives if asked to; refusal to do so could be punished by imprisonment.

Thoreau and other abolitionists were furious. Even the gentle Emerson vowed he would disobey the law. Thoreau soon had a chance to act. On September 30, 1851, Henry Williams, an escaped slave who had been living in Boston, learned there was a warrant out for his arrest. With a letter of introduction from Garrison, he walked the 20 miles to the Thoreaus' house in Concord. There he was lodged until Henry bought him a ticket and got him on a train bound for northern Vermont the next day. From there Williams made his way to Canada. Later Thoreau and other antislavery people raised money to buy Williams's freedom which enabled him to come back to Boston. Soon after his return as a free man, Williams again walked to Concord; this time to present Thoreau with a statue of Uncle Tom and Eva, central characters in Harriet Beecher Stowe's widely read antislavery novel, *Uncle Tom's Cabin*.

Successes such as Thoreau's with Williams, of course, in no way diminished the tenacity of the slaveholders. As the 1850s progressed, the South grew more rash. Meanwhile northern abolitionists became increasingly frustrated. In 1854 Congress passed the Kansas-Nebraska Act. This highly controversial measure created a new Kansas Territory west of Missouri, overturned an earlier congressional ban on slavery in that area, and opened up the territory to settlers bringing slaves. Kansas quickly became a battleground as pro- and anti-slavery forces fought for dominance. Thoreau and other Northerners soon were reading of the exploits of John Brown, one of the leaders of the antislavery guerrilla forces fighting for the freedom of Kansas.

In 1854, Boston itself became a battleground. On May 24, Anthony Burns, a fugitive slave living in Boston, was arrested. A group of abolitionists led by Thomas Wentworth Higginson made an unsuccessful attempt at rescue. Massachusetts authorities, in compliance with the Fugitive Slave Law, called out the state militia. Under heavily armed guard they escorted Burns to Boston's Long Wharf and shipped him back to Virginia and slavery. Twelve of the abolitionists who had tried to rescue Burns were jailed.

Enraged by the willingness of the government of Massachusetts to assist the slaveowner and thereby condone slavery, Thoreau denounced that government in a stinging essay, "Slavery in Massachusetts." This he delivered on the Fourth of July in Framingham, Massachusetts. Referring to the robbing of "a poor innocent black man of his liberty for life" as a "moral earthquake," he warned, "my thoughts are murder to the State." In language much harsher than "Civil Disobedience" he denounced the expediency of the politicians:

> There is no such thing as accomplishing a righteous reform by the use of "expediency." There is no such thing as sliding up hill. In morals the only sliders are backsliders . . . Will mankind never learn that policy is not morality,—that it never secures any moral right, but considers merely what is expedient? chooses the available candidate,—who is invariably the Devil,—and what right have his constituents to be surprised, because the Devil does not behave like an angel of light? What is wanted is men, not of policy, but of probity,—who recognize a higher law than the Constitution, or the decision of the majority.

In "Slavery in Massachusetts" Thoreau blamed not only the state and its servile politicians for sanctioning slavery, but pulpit and press as well. He accused the church of the same compromise and complacency as that practiced by the state. But it was the press, he claimed, that was the most corrupt. "No country was ever ruled by so mean a class of tyrants as, with a few noble exceptions, are the editors of the periodical press in *this* country. And as they live and rule only by their servility, and appealing to the worse, and not the better, nature of man, the people who read them are in the condition of the dog that returns to his vomit."

The abolitionists present at Thoreau's speech were deeply moved; nor did its influence stop there. The *Anti-Slavery Standard* published a shortened version of the address, while Garrison's *Liberator* and Greeley's New York *Tribune* published the complete text.

Yet despite this vigorous and well-publicized denunciation, slavery continued, North and South drew further apart and Thoreau became more despondent. In a letter to an English friend, Thomas Cholmondeley, he wrote: "There has not been anything which you could call union between the North and South in this country for many years, and there cannot be so long as slavery is in the way. I only wish that Northern—that any men—were better material, or that I for one had more skill to deal with them; that the north had more spirit and would settle the question at once, and here instead of struggling feebly and protractedly away off on the plains of Kansas."

Thoreau and many other abolitionists were growing impatient and more militant. Though he himself realized his strength lay in the pen and not the sword, he was ready to support someone who could take sword in hand and smite the southern slaveholders. He found such a man in John Brown.

A tall, strong, sinewy, and ceremonious man with penetrating bluish-gray eyes, John Brown had a depth and purpose in his demeanor. His bearded face was weather-beaten from years of fighting against slavery in Kansas. In 1857 and again in 1859 he came to New England to raise money and support for his guerrilla forces. On both occasions he spoke in Concord and had long talks with Thoreau. Here was a man with a higher purpose in life than mere material acquisition; a man willing to risk his life for the slaves' freedom. Henry was impressed and contributed a small sum to his cause. Thoreau described him as "a man of rare common sense and directness of speech, as of action; a transcendentalist above all, a man of ideas and principles,—that was what distinguished him. Not yielding to a whim or transient impulse, but carrying out the purpose of a life."

In mid-October, 1859, John Brown and his band of 18 men, five of them black, raided the United States arsenal at Harper's Ferry in Virginia. This bold effort to start a war of liberation ended in failure. Brown and most of his men were killed or executed.

Thoreau, who knew nothing in advance of Brown's plans, was with Alcott at Emerson's house on October 19, when word of Harper's Ferry and Brown's arrest reached him. He immediately came to Brown's defense and for the next few weeks he poured his thoughts about this "superior man" into his journal. So absorbed was he with Brown that he was "surprised whenever I detected the routine of the natural world surviving still."

Not regularly a newspaper reader, Thoreau read all the papers he could after the event. He was appalled to find the press dismissing Brown as a mad, fanatical fool. Even the abolitionist press reacted negatively. Garrison's *Liberator* labeled the raid "a misguided, wild, and apparently insane—effort." To Thoreau, such reactions revealed a lack of principle. "Many, no doubt, are well disposed," he wrote, "but sluggish by constitution and by habit, and they cannot conceive of a man who is actuated by higher motives than they are. Accordingly they pronounce this man insane, for they know that they could never act as he does, as long as they are themselves."

In an effort to set the record straight Thoreau announced that he would speak on John Brown in the Concord town hall on October 30. Once more the selectmen refused to ring the town bell. Thoreau again rang it himself and then delivered a most eloquent speech, "A Plea for Captain John Brown." "Little as I know of Captain Brown," he told his audience, "I would fain do my part to correct the tone and statements of the newspapers, and of my countrymen generally, respecting his character and actions. It costs us nothing to be just. We can at least express our sympathy with, and admiration of, him and his companions, and that is what I now propose to do." Comparing Brown to the brave Minutemen who stood at Concord's North Bridge at the start of the Revolution, he rejoiced that he lived "in this age, that I am his contemporary." Thoreau looked forward to a time when Brown's attack on Harper's Ferry would be celebrated as a great part of America's national heritage: "The poet will sing it; the historian record it; and, with the Landing of the Pilgrims and the Declaration of Independence, it will be the ornament of some future national gallery, when at least the present form of slavery shall be no more here. We shall then be at liberty to weep for Captain Brown. Then, and not till then, we will take our revenge."

The next day Thoreau received a telegram asking him to repeat the lecture on November 1, at Boston's Tremont Temple, the city's largest auditorium. Frederick Douglass, the great black abolitionist, had been the scheduled speaker, but since Douglass was a known confidant of Brown it had been necessary for him to flee to Canada to avoid arrest. Thoreau accepted the invitation and was greeted with great applause before a packed house. Two days later he repeated the lecture in Worcester. On December 2, Brown was hanged. In a memorial service that Thoreau arranged that day in Concord he delivered another moving tribute: the "Martyrdom of John Brown." The following summer Thoreau wrote "The Last Days of John

Brown" to be read at a Fourth of July memorial held at Brown's final burial site in North Elba, New York.

John Brown in 1854. (Library of Congress)

Thoreau's zeal for Brown has bothered many scholars. How could this noted champion of non-violent resistance to injustice support an armed uprising? Such critics fail to place Thoreau's championing of Brown into an historic context. He was not alone in coming to see violence as the solution. Years of peaceful propaganda by antislavery people had not shaken the determination of the slaveholders to hold on to their slaves. Antislavery leaders such as Douglass, Theodore Parker, Angelina Grimké, and many more were reluctantly learning, in Douglass's words, that it may be necessary "to fight the devil with fire."

Thoreau and thousands like him were really following in the footsteps of the revolutionaries of '76. They had come to the

0

conclusion that when government became destructive of the people's natural rights then the people had the right to rebel. "It was his peculiar doctrine," wrote Thoreau of Brown, "that a man has a perfect right to interfere by force with the slaveholder, in order to rescue the slave. I agree with him." In this sense, Thoreau's support of Brown's use of force was really not that different from pacifists like Garrison supporting the Civil War as a means of ending slavery, and this Garrison and most pacifists did.

But while Thoreau was not unique in his coming to regard violence as sometimes necessary, he was among the first to recognize the larger significance of Harper's Ferry. Brown had told Frederick Douglass before his raid that he wished to do "something startling" in an effort "to rouse the nation." Harper's Ferry, he had predicted, would be a trumpet blast to rally the friends of freedom. It did just that. Brown's attack touched off events that ultimately began the Civil War that would end American slavery.

Thoreau had been one of the earliest of Brown's defenders. After Brown's death, however, millions of Northerners came to see him as a martyr, and when the Civil War began, Union troops marched to battle singing:

> John Brown's body lies a moldering in the grave.
> John Brown's body lies a moldering in the grave.
> John Brown's body lies a moldering in the grave.
> His truth goes marching on!

Both Brown and Thoreau had been vindicated, though neither lived to see the end of slavery.

9
THE LAST YEARS

That Walt Whitman, of whom I wrote to
you, is the most interesting fact to me at
present. I have just read his 2nd edition
(which he gave me) and it has done me
more good than any reading for a long
time. Perhaps I remember best the poem
of Walt Whitman an American & the Sun
Down Poem . . . He is a great fellow.
—Letter to Harrison Blake, Dec. 7, 1856

While Thoreau's forays into the public arena brought him
occasionally to the forefront of antislavery agitation,
most of his days were spent in the same pleasing pattern
he had developed as a young man. As he noted in his Journal in
1853, "I spend the forenoon in my chamber, writing or arranging
my papers, and in the afternoon I walk forth into the fields and
woods. I turn aside, perchance, into some withdrawn, untrodden
swamp, and find these bilberries, large and fair, awaiting me in
inexhaustible abundance, for I have no tame garden."

Thoreau's obsession with the natural world intensified into
a scientific study in the last decade of his life. His voluminous
Journals during the 1850s included detailed listings of all the
trees, flowers, and plants in the vicinity of Concord, together
with information on their times of leafing and flowering, their
patterns of growth, and their methods of seed dispersal. He
kept careful accounts of birds and animals with descriptions of
their tracks, nests, and habitats, and dates they were sighted.
He recorded water and pond temperatures and levels as well
as a vast amount of information about the weather. The totality
of his natural observations set him apart from naturalists of
his day and have led modern scholars to hail him as a pioneer

ecologist concerned with the whole environment and its inter-relatedness.

Thoreau came to regard nature as ever changing rather than as a fixed single entity. This view made it easy for him to embrace Charles Darwin's theory of evolution, which he did upon reading Darwin's *Origin of Species* in 1860. "The development theory," he wrote, "implies a greater vital force in nature, because it is more flexible and accommodating, and equivalent to a sort of constant new creation."

After the publication of *Walden* in 1854, writing in his Journal became his major occupation, his way of relating himself to nature. The Concord countryside was his microcosm, a window to understand the larger world. He hoped someday to write a book on the natural history of Concord and to reveal its organic harmony. He wished to study its natural phenomena with the skills of the scientist and the eyes of the poet, to combine minute observation with aesthetic insight. "Nature," he wrote, "is reported not by him who goes forth consciously as an observer, but in the fullness of life. To such a one she rushes to make her report. To the full heart she is all but a figure of speech."

Unfortunately, he never lived to complete this project, to create the final unity of vision out of his years of examination. But he did leave a vast, remarkable Journal, which, although lacking in overall artistic unity, is rich, vital and frequently brilliant. Though the Journal's more than two million words are intimidating, for the patient reader its rewards are immense. Not only will such a reader come upon some of Thoreau's best writing, but he or she will also gain a closer knowledge of the private man.

During these post-Walden years of intensive nature study and Journal keeping, Thoreau lived at home and helped his father when needed in the pencil business. He also found frequent employment as a surveyor. There was an irony in his taking up this occupation, as Thoreau often surveyed local woodlots prior to their sale to lumbermen—a sale he presumably regretted. Yet it was employment that kept him out-of-doors and left him his independence. He even hired his former jailer, Sam Staples, as his rodman.

Surveying occasionally took Thoreau away from Concord. His furthest job-related trip occurred in the fall of 1856, when he was hired to survey Eagleswood, an experimental community on the New Jersey coast near Perth Amboy. Among the residents there were many well-known abolitionists, reformers and Quakers. Thoreau as usual was not impressed by communal life, though he did delight the children there with his tales of the Maine woods.

While working at Eagleswood, Thoreau made several trips to New York City, accompanied by Bronson Alcott. He visited his old friend, Horace Greeley, and several other acquaintances. But most memorable was his meeting Walt Whitman.

Like Thoreau, Whitman as a young man had come under the spell of Emersonian transcendentalism. He, too, loved nature and aspired to be the great American poet. A year before his meeting with Thoreau, Whitman had published a slim volume of poems entitled *Leaves of Grass*. This was a new kind of poetry, a sensual celebration of self, nature, and humanity, a

Walt Whitman as he appeared on the frontispiece of the first edition of Leaves of Grass *in 1855.* (Author's collection)

poetry of democracy. The initial edition of *Leaves of Grass* was even more of a commercial failure than Thoreau's first book. But Whitman sent a copy of the book to Emerson who, in a glowing letter back, praised *Leaves* as "the most extraordinary piece of wit and wisdom that America has yet contributed . . . I greet you at the beginning of a great career." Whitman, without consulting Emerson, circulated this letter to publishers and critics and then arranged a second edition of *Leaves* to be printed with the "I greet you" sentence and Emerson's name stamped on the book's spine in gold letters.

Thoreau and Alcott were introduced to Whitman by acquaintances of the poet and visited him in his Brooklyn bedroom which also served as his study. The bed was unmade, the chamber pot was in view, and there were unframed pictures of Bacchus, Hercules and a satyr pinned to the wall which led Alcott to ask: "Which, now of the three, particularly, is the new poet here—this Hercules, the Bacchus, or the satyr?" Whitman refused to answer. They conversed for several hours, and Thoreau, who had already read the first edition of *Leaves of Grass*, was fascinated. He gave Whitman a copy of *A Week*. Whitman in turn gave him the revised 1856 edition of *Leaves* with Emerson's congratulatory sentence.

On his return to Concord, Thoreau could talk of little else besides Whitman. In letters to his friend, Harrison Blake, he called Whitman "the greatest democrat the world has seen," and said "he has spoken more truth than any American or modern that I know. I have found his poems exhilarating encouraging."

Whitman appears to have been less excited by Thoreau than was Henry by him. Yet over the years the Camden poet came to admire the Concord rebel: "One thing about Thoreau keeps him very near to me," he wrote, "I refer to his lawlessness—his dissent—his going his own absolute road let hell blaze all it chooses." In 1888 the aging poet concluded "Thoreau belongs to America, to the transcendental, to the protesters . . . he was a force—he looms up bigger and bigger: his dying does not seem to have hurt him a bit: every year has added to his fame."

At the time of their 1856 meeting, Thoreau was 39, two years older than the poet. But while Whitman would survive until 1892 and come to be recognized as America's foremost poet, Henry Thoreau would live less than six more years and would be long dead before being widely praised as a truly great author.

Thoreau with a full beard the year before his death. (Author's collection)

Thoreau suffered from frequent colds and more serious respiratory problems that were aggravated by the graphite dust that filled the Thoreau house from the attached pencil-making factory. In 1855, the year before his meeting with Whitman, he came down with an undiagnosed illness that so weakened him he had to discontinue his regular walks for several months. Then in early December, 1860, after being outside on a damp wintery day counting tree rings, he came down with a bad cold that soon developed into bronchitis. He was bedridden most of the remaining winter.

In the spring of 1861 the firing on Fort Sumter began the Civil War, but Thoreau was too ill to take much interest. Hoping that a change of climate would improve his health, he decided to take a trip. For reasons unclear, local doctors were mistakenly touting the Middle West as having air that was dry and easy on the lungs. In May, 1861, Thoreau set out for Minnesota, accompanied by 17-year-old Horace Mann, Jr., the son of the famous educational reformer. The two men saw some Sioux Indians; the Mississippi; Mackinac Island, Michigan; and some wild apple trees, but the trip was of no benefit to Thoreau's health. When the travelers returned to Concord that July, Thoreau's condition had become worse.

That fall and winter, as the war between North and South escalated, Thoreau continued to weaken. His bronchitis had turned to tuberculosis, a disease which today is almost unknown in the United States, but then was a very common killer. His last Journal entry was made on November 3, recording the playful antics of kittens and the visible aftertraces of storms. He asked that his bed be brought from his attic room to the parlor so that he might share the company of family and friends. He also continued to work, revising essays and books for publication, and when he was no longer able to write he dictated to his sister, Sophia.

Many came to visit Thoreau during his last months and were surprised at his high spirits. Sam Staples claimed never to have seen a dying man "with so much pleasure and peace." When his Aunt Louisa asked if he had made his peace with God, he replied, "I did not know we had ever quarreled, Aunt." A few days before his death, Parker Pillsbury, an abolitionist and family friend, seeing how sickly Thoreau appeared asked: "You seem so near the brink of the dark river, that I almost wonder how the opposite shore may appear to you." With scarcely audible voice the dying man answered: "One world at a time." Quietly and without apparent pain, Henry Thoreau died on the morning of May 6,

1862. He would have been 45 that July. His last audible words were "moose" and "Indian."[1]

Plans were made for a public funeral to be held at the First Parish Church, even though Thoreau had officially "signed off" from the church as a young man. A little before 3:00 on the afternoon of May 9, the bells tolled and the church filled to capacity. Friends such as Channing, Alcott, and Hawthorne were present. His friend, Emerson, in a "broken, tender voice" delivered an extensive eulogy:

> No truer American existed than Thoreau . . . He was of short stature, firmly built, of light complexion, with strong, serious blue eyes, and a grave aspect,—his face covered in the late years with a becoming beard. His senses were acute, his frame well-knit and hardy, his hands strong and skilful in the use of tools. And there was a wonderful fitness of body and mind. He could pace sixteen rods more accurately than another man could measure them with rod and chain. He could find his path in the woods at night, he said, better by his feet than his eyes. He could estimate the measure of a tree very well by his eye; he could estimate the weight of a calf or a pig, like a dealer. From a box containing a bushel or more of loose pencils, he could take up with his hands fast enough just a dozen pencils at every grasp. He was a good swimmer, runner, skater, boatman, and would probably outwalk most countrymen in a day's journey. And the relation of body to mind was still finer than we have indicated.

Emerson concluded, "His soul was made for the noblest society; he had in a short life exhausted the capabilities of this world; wherever there is knowledge, wherever there is virtue, wherever there is beauty, he will find a home."

He was buried in the family plot in the New Burying Ground. Years later the body was moved to nearby Sleepy Hollow Cemetery and marked with a stone stating simply "HENRY." Close by are the graves of Alcott, Channing, Emerson, and Hawthorne.

---

[1]At the time of Thoreau's death the Confederate commander, General Joseph Johnston, was retreating in Virginia before General George McClellan's Union troops. East of Williamsburg the land, in its spring mantle, was littered with corpses.

10

EPILOGUE

> I am disappointed to find that most that I
> am and value myself for is lost, or worse
> than lost, on my audience. I fail to get even
> the attention of the mass. I should suit
> them better if I suited myself less. I feel
> that the public demand an average
> man—average thoughts and manners—not
> originality, nor even absolute excellence.
> You cannot interest them except as you are
> like them and sympathize with them. I
> would rather that my audience come to me
> than that I should go to them . . .
> —*Journal*, December 6, 1854

At the time of his death Thoreau had a small, devoted
following, but only slight national recognition. His
reputation would grow quickly. In the summer of 1862
Ticknor and Fields reissued both *Walden* and *A Week*. Thoreau's
beautiful essay on wilderness entitled "Walking" was the
lead article in the June *Atlantic Monthly*: within the next
two and a half years that highly respected literary magazine
would publish seven more of Thoreau's nature and travel
articles.

The *Atlantic* also published Emerson's funeral oration and
a tribute to Thoreau by Bronson Alcott entitled "The For-
ester." Thoreau was a great hero to Alcott: "I know of nothing
more creditable to his greatness than the thoughtful regard,
approaching to reverence by which he has been held for many
years by some of the best persons of his time, living at a
distance, and wont to make their annual pilgrimage, usually

on foot, to the master . . . Pan is dead, and Nature ailing throughout."

In 1863 Ticknor and Fields brought out a collection of Thoreau's travel essays under the title *Excursions in Field and Forest*. This was followed by *The Maine Woods* in 1864; *Cape Cod* and a collection of *Letters to Various Persons* in 1865; and *A Yankee in Canada with Anti-Slavery and Reform Papers* in 1866. Eleven years after his death Ellery Channing published the first book-length biography, *Thoreau: The Poet-Naturalist*. In 1882, another friend and the person who introduced Thoreau to John Brown, Franklin B. Sanborn, contributed *Henry D. Thoreau* to the "American Men of Letters" series.

Despite this exposure, Thoreau's reputation in the later 19th century was not uniformly good. Poet Oliver Wendell Holmes, for instance, though admitting Thoreau's "many rare and admirable qualities," called him a "nullifier of civilization, who insisted on nibbling his asparagus at the wrong end." John Greenleaf Whittier claimed that Thoreau was "a man willing to sink himself into a woodchuck." To Robert Louis Stevenson he was a "skulker." Critic James Russell Lowell dismissed Thoreau as having an unhealthy mind and no sense of humor, "he condemns a world, the hollowness of whose satisfactions he had never had the means of testing." In general such critics saw Thoreau as an anti-social egotist and a crank, or as simply a minor imitator of Emerson.

Such attacks were not the only barrier to the growth of Thoreau's reputation after his death. The Civil War and the rapid urbanization and industrialization of the post–Civil War years drove transcendentalism out of style. Literature in the late 19th century came to be dominated by a frank realism and an even harsher naturalism. Romantic transcendental writings with their emphasis on the spirituality of nature now seemed old-fashioned.

Yet Thoreau's reputation survived these obstacles, and with each passing decade he attracted more readers. By the 1880s and 1890s many Americans came to realize that the century's vast economic growth had produced a wasteland: nature, in America, was being raped. In 1890 the Census Bureau announced the end of the frontier. Suddenly there was a flood of interest in nature. By the early 20th century this interest had turned into the beginnings of a national movement for conservation. Thoreau now began to be recognized as America's foremost nature writer, a reputation furthered by his friend, Harrison Blake, who between 1881 and 1892 published four volumes of selections from the Journal, named after the seasons.

Thoreau's growing reputation was not limited to America. In 1890 Englishman Henry Salt published the best biography of Thoreau to that time. During the 1890s the Fabian socialists, the intellectual founders of the British Labour party, helped popularize *Walden* and "Civil Disobedience." Local Labour party units were even referred to as Walden Clubs. In 1897, Frederick van Eeden established a utopian community named Walden outside of Amsterdam, Holland; in 1902 he sponsored a Dutch translation of Thoreau's classic. In Russia the great novelist, Leo Tolstoy, called Thoreau one of "a bright constellation" of American writers, "who . . . specially influenced me." Tolstoy chastised Americans for paying more attention to "financial and industrial millionaires or successful generals" than to the genius of Thoreau.

Houghton Mifflin's publication of a 20-volume collection of Thoreau's writings in 1906, marked his recognition as part of the accepted canon of great American authors. These volumes made possible the growth of a new scholarship devoted to the study of Thoreau.

Most Americans continued to think of Thoreau as a nature writer only. Not until 1927, with the publication of Vernon L. Parrington's pathbreaking *Main Currents in American Thought* did large numbers of people recognize Thoreau as a social and political thinker as well. And not until F. O. Matthiessen, the renowned Harvard scholar, published *American Renaissance* in 1941 was attention turned toward the brilliance of Thoreau's literary craftsmanship, especially in *Walden*.

Despite the great recognition Thoreau has received in the 20th century, he has remained a controversial figure. Earlier in the century radical intellectuals Emma Goldman, Upton Sinclair, and Norman Thomas were arrested for reading from "Civil Disobedience" in public. In the 1950s infamous, anticommunist witch-hunter Senator Joseph McCarthy succeeded in having Thoreau's writings removed from United States Information Service libraries throughout the world. Even after the U.S. government recognized Thoreau in 1967 on the 150th anniversary of his birth with a commemorative postage stamp, Senator Robert Byrd of West Virginia protested against honoring a man "who had a thoroughly anti-social personality."

Yet for each 20th-century debunker there appear to be thousands of Thoreau enthusiasts worldwide. Today *Walden* is available in literally hundreds of editions in virtually every language. It has been reprinted more than any other pre–Civil War American book. In Japan, for instance, where many find Thoreau's thoughts close to that of Zen Buddhists, there have been at least 15 translations of *Walden*.

He is a writer who generates strong feelings. Many individuals in this century have confessed a deep indebtedness to him. Some have even claimed him as a regenerative, life-changing force who has given them spiritual awareness and an appreciation of the variety of life's possibilities.

Thoreau is not an easy writer to classify. He did not write novels; he was not strictly speaking a philosopher; nor was he purely a naturalist, travel writer or social reformer. Yet he was more than any of these separate categories suggest—a writer the likes of whom the country had never seen before, nor since. His writings have a richness and depth comparable to the splendid scriptures and mythologies of ancient civilizations that he was so fond of reading.

Today Henry Thoreau is universally acknowledged as one of America's greatest writers whose prose at its best has seldom been equaled. His message becomes more significant with the passage of time. During the depression years of the 1930s, for example, Thoreau seemed to speak directly to the problems of an industrial society gone bankrupt. In the period of the protest movements of the 1950s and 1960s, he inspired legions of civil rights activists, antiwar demonstrators, and advocates of a counterculture. In our own age of crude materialism, conformity, and global concerns about environmental catastrophe and omnipotent technology he speaks to millions.

In his day he spoke for a humane and peaceful world; one free from the curses of materialism, elitism, racism, and war; one lived in simplicity and in harmony with nature. If our planet is to survive to celebrate the bicentennial of his death in the year 2062, the world would do well to heed his vision.

SELECTED BIBLIOGRAPHY

The 20-volume compilation of *The Writings of Henry David Thoreau* (1906), edited by Bradford Torrey, remains the standard edition for serious Thoreau scholars. Princeton University Press is in the process of publishing what promises to be a definitive collection of Thoreau's writings. When this is finished it will supersede the Torrey edition. *Walden and Other Writings* (1981), edited by William Howarth, is an excellent one-volume anthology, though students should be forewarned that it includes abridged versions of *A Week on the Concord and Merrimack Rivers, Cape Cod*, and *The Maine Woods*. Walter Harding, ed., *The Variorum Walden* (1962), and J. Lyndon Shanley, ed., *Walden* (1971), are excellent annotated editions of Thoreau's classic. Shanley has also written *The Making of Walden* (1957) showing how the book developed through successive revisions.

Any serious student of Thoreau should read his Journal. But for those put off by its length—14 massive volumes in the Torrey edition—Odell Shepard has edited a slim volume, *The Heart of Thoreau's Journals* (1961 ed.). Also drawn largely from the Journal is Helen Cruickshank, ed., *Thoreau on Birds* (1964), a delightful compilation of Thoreau's ornithological writings. *The Correspondence of Henry David Thoreau* (1958), edited by Carl Bode and Walter Harding, is also important for students of Thoreau. Carl Bode has also edited Thoreau's *Collected Poems* (1964).

The most detailed and factually reliable biography of Thoreau is Walter Harding, *The Days of Henry Thoreau* (1982 ed.). More interpretive, though less accurate, versions of Thoreau's life are: Joseph Wood Krutch, *Henry David Thoreau* (1948), and Henry S. Canby *Thoreau* (1939). Richard Lebeaux's *Young Man Thoreau* (1977) and *Thoreau's Seasons* (1984) are interesting psychological interpretations of Thoreau's early and later life respectively. Useful for their anecdotes, though generally unreliable, are the early accounts by Thoreau's friends: William Ellery Channing, *Thoreau: The Poet-Naturalist* (1873), and Franklin B. Sanborn, *The Life of Henry David Thoreau* (1882). A delightful reminiscence by Ralph Waldo Emerson's son is: Edward Waldo Emerson, *Henry Thoreau as Remembered by a Young Friend* (1917).

A helpful guide to Thoreau scholarship is Walter Harding and Michael Meyer, *The New Thoreau Handbook* (1980). The *Thoreau Society Bulletin* (1941–) lists current items in each quarterly issue. There are also two other journals devoted to Thoreau: *The Concord Saunterer* (1966–); and the *Thoreau Journal Quarterly* (1969–).

A fine study of Thoreau's intellectual development as a transcendentalist and artist is Sherman Paul, *The Shores of America: Thoreau's Inward Exploration* (1958). Robert D. Richardson's *Henry David Thoreau: A Life of the Mind* (1986) is a frustratingly fragmented book that nevertheless does a good job of placing Thoreau into a larger cultural context. Other worthwhile recent studies are: Richard J. Schneider, *Henry David Thoreau* (1987); Edward Wagenknecht, *Henry David Thoreau* (1981); and William Howarth, *The Book of Concord: Thoreau's Life as a Writer* (1982).

Collections of critical essays are: Harold Bloom, ed., *Henry David Thoreau* (1987); Walter Harding, ed., *Henry David Thoreau: A Profile* (1971); Wendell Glick, ed., *The Recognition of Henry David Thoreau* (1970); John H. Hicks, ed., *Thoreau in Our Season* (1966); and Sherman Paul, ed., *Thoreau: A Collection of Critical Essays* (1962).

Thoreau's social and economic criticisms are the subject of Leonard N. Neufeldt, *The Economist: Henry Thoreau and Enterprise* (1989); Taylor Stoehr, *Nay-Saying in Concord* (1979); and Leo Stoller, *After Walden: Thoreau's Changing Views of Economic Man* (1957).

Specific changes in Massachusetts social and economic life during Thoreau's time are treated in: Jonathan Prude, *Coming of Industrial Order: Town and Factory Life in Rural Massachusetts, 1810–1860* (1983); and Jack Larkin, *The Reshaping of Everyday Life, 1760–1860* (1988). For a broader view of America's modernization, see Douglas T. Miller's *The Birth of Modern America, 1820–1850* (1970), and *Then Was the Future: The North in the Age of Jackson, 1815–1850* (1973). The standard history of Thoreau's Concord is Ruth R. Wheeler, *Concord: Climate for Freedom* (1967).

Thoreau's interest in nature is best discussed in James McIntosh's *Thoreau as Romantic Naturalist: His Shifting Stance toward Nature* (1974). Also insightful are: John Hildebidle, *Thoreau: A Naturalist's Liberty* (1983); Joan Burbick, *Thoreau's Alternative History: Changing Perspectives on Nature, Culture, and Language* (1987); Reginald Cook, *Passage to Walden* (1958); and Sharon Cameron, *Writing Nature: Henry Thoreau's Journal* (1985). Roderick Nash, *Wilderness and the American Mind* (1967), shows Thoreau to have been a significant, pioneer conservationist and ecologist.

Robert Sayre, *Thoreau and the American Indians* (1977), is a fine analysis of Thoreau's attitudes toward American Indians. Also of interest is Richard F. Fleck, *Henry Thoreau and John Muir among the Indians* (1985).

Joel Porte's *Emerson and Thoreau: Transcendentalists in Conflict* (1965) helps understand these two friends' complex relationship. Lawrence Buell, *Literary Transcendentalism: Style and Vision in the American Renaissance* (1973), places Thoreau into the larger context of New England transcendentalism.

Useful articles on aspects of Thoreau's life and literature include: Joseph Allen Boone, "Delving and Diving for Truth: Breaking through to Bottom in Thoreau's *Walden.*" *ESQ: A Journal of the American Renaissance*, 27, No. 3 (1981). 135–146; Philip Gura, "Thoreau's Maine Woods Indians: More Representative Men," *American Literature*, 49 (November, 1977), 366–384; Melvin E. Lyon, "Walden Pond as Symbol," *PLMA*, 82 (May, 1967), 289–300; Michael Meyer, "Thoreau's Rescue of John Brown from History," in *Studies in the American Renaissance 1980*, 301–316; Walter Benn Michaels, "*Walden*'s False Bottoms," *Glyph*, 1 (1977), 132–149; and Lorrie Smith, "Walking from England to America: Re-Viewing Thoreau's Romanticism," *New England Quarterly*, 58, No. 2 (June, 1985), 221–241.

Finally, the changes in Thoreau's critical reputation over the years are surveyed in Wendell Glick, *The Recognition of Henry David Thoreau* (1969), and Michael Meyer, *Several More Lives to Live: Thoreau's Political Reputation in America* (1977).

INDEX

Italic numbers indicate illustrations